WHATEVER THE YEARS

ALSO BY RONALD SELBY WRIGHT:

LONGMANS GREEN:

The Average Man—Broadcast Talks
The Greater Victory—Broadcast Talks
Small Talks—Broadcast Talks

OLIVER AND BOYD:

Let's Ask the Padre—Broadcast Talks
The Padre Presents—Broadcast Discussions

OXFORD UNIVERSITY PRESS:

(with A. W. Loos) *Asking Why*—Broadcast Discussions
A Short Outline of the Christian Faith (in preparation)

EDITED:

OXFORD UNIVERSITY PRESS:

Asking them Questions—First Series
Asking them Questions—Second Series
Soldiers Also Asked
Asking them Questions—Third Series (in preparation)

ALLENSON:

I Attack

HODDER AND STOUGHTON:

Front Line Religion
Studdert-Kennedy's *Why Aren't All the Best Chaps Christians?*

Frontispiece

Photo by Charles J. Chislett, A.R.P.S.

The Author (left) and Roy King at Hitler's house, Berchtesgaten

WHATEVER THE YEARS

by

RONALD SELBY WRIGHT

THE EPWORTH PRESS
(Edgar C. Barton)
25-35 City Road, London, E.C.1

PRINTED IN GREAT BRITAIN
BY WESTERN PRINTING SERVICES LTD., BRISTOL

Dedication

TO

ROYSTON M. KING
THE ROYAL CORPS OF SIGNALS

MY DEAR ROY,

This little book is a promise fulfilled; for you may remember how, in Trieste, I said that the next book of talks I wrote I'd dedicate to you (as if you hadn't heard enough of them already!) and associate it too with Pat Garrett. This now I gladly do, as a token of friendship through that last year of war and the first glorious months of peace, when hearts had lightened and the sun shone bright for a time and fear vanished with the dawn of peace, and, for a time, we felt that it was going to be well with the world. So we bathed at Sistiana and Grado, rode through Venice in a gondola, ate water melons on a British warship in Trieste harbour, laughed our way through Europe with Charlie and George, or read Rupert Brooke by my caravan beside the Isonso River. And sometimes we discussed the years of war and hoped they had not been wasted years. Because with all their destruction, and fear, and horror, they had brought, too, so much that was rich and valuable.

A war that began so wonderfully in friendship with men like Ronnie Alexander, Bobbie Gunn, John Chiene, Charlie Herriot, Hugh Rose, Ivor Salvesen, Walter Scott, David Haddon, Charles Findlay, Hugh Johnston, John McKee, F. L. Johnston, Jack Hankey, 'Chokra' Kelly, General 'Jim' Cassels, Sir Neil Ritchie; and M.O.s like Jimmy Mason-Brown, Graeme Warrack, John Newton, and Hilary Dorman; and Padres like Joe Gray, Nevile Davidson, Willie Tindall, Jimmie Wood, Bernard Haddelsey and Pat Stevenson—a war that began like that had then for me a very bad patch when I nearly lost faith in the friendship of man. And this you and Pat restored to me and began for me a grand 'finish'—the meeting again of my old boys of Club and camp days—Stanley McLean, George Flannigan, Harry Holt, Andrew Bell; and then there's 'Crackers' May of the Durham Light Infantry, Walter Goodman, Brian Daunt, General Denys Reid, Terence Smith, and Padres like John Marshall, Adam Macpherson, Allan MacArthur, Robin Woods, Tom Torrance, and the one and only Duncan McGillivray, as well as T. M. Layng and Victor Pike—whom I have mentioned elsewhere. Whatever the years have taken, they have left these and many other precious names. And with them the glorious memory of those who were 'called home'—Jimmie Dalgleish, Jack Cropper, Billy Brown, Jim Stewart, Davie Adams, Joe Ewart, Jim Stobbie—so many other precious names who are in the hands of God, 'where no torment can touch them'.

The tomorrow we talked about yesterday has not yet come, yet I know that you—and countless thousands like you—believe that 'there are glorious days ahead, if we choose to make them glorious'. And, whatever the years have taken, they have, as I have said, also given; not only in the priceless gifts of friendship, but in a realization that often when things are at their worst, man is at his best; when the fight seemed lost, we became the more determined to win through; and when we stood alone against the forces of evil, the greatest man of our age, with a promise of 'blood, and sweat, and tears', led us to our 'finest hour'.

Whatever the years have taken, they have given us the clue, would we but see it, of winning not only a war but a peace—'to give and not to count the cost, to fight and not

to heed the wounds, to toil and not to seek for rest, to labour
and not to ask for any reward'. But first, remember:
'Teach us, O Lord, to serve Thee, as Thou deservest.'

RONALD SELBY WRIGHT

ACHESON HOUSE
THE MANSE OF THE CANONGATE
EDINBURGH, 8
Pentecost 1946

WHATEVER THE YEARS HAVE TAKEN, *they have given you a comradeship that shall endure. To share hardship, to struggle side by side against great odds, to look death in the face, and, above all, to talk together, sometimes, of the Tomorrow you risked your lives to win —these are things that bind you in a fellowship that must not pass away.*

LESLIE F. CHURCH

Note

SOME OF these talks were broadcast to the Eighth Army and Desert Air Force in Italy and Austria and on the Scottish and Overseas Services of the B.B.C. Parts of some, too, have appeared in *The Eighth Army News*, *The Union Jack*, *The Diaconals*, *The Sunday Chronicle*, *The Edinburgh Evening News*, *The Sword*, *The Scottish Forces Magazine*, and *The Canongate Chronicle*.

I have departed from my usual publisher in order to have the honour of being associated with my friend Dr. Leslie F. Church, the Editor of The Epworth Press. It was a great joy to meet him in Italy; and in addition to his visit being a much-needed tonic to us all, I heard him preach what, I think, is the greatest sermon I've heard.

In addition to thanking Dr. Church for his kind interest in this book, I should also like to thank my good friends Mr. Melville Dinwiddie, C.B.E., the Scottish Director of the B.B.C., and the Rev. Ronald Falconer, their Scottish Religious Assistant, for their ever helpful advice; and last, but by no means least, two of the greatest Padres I've ever met—under whom it was my privilege to serve—the Rev. T. M. Layng, C.B.E., M.C., Deputy Chaplain-General, C.M.F., and the Rev. Victor Pike, O.B.E., Assistant Chaplain-General, Eighth Army, and now Deputy Chaplain-General M.E.F., whose inspiring leadership and happy friendship made the brotherhood of Chaplains in Italy and Austria a wonderful reality.

R.S.W.

Contents

Illustrations

One

Prologue

A BETTER MORNING—IF

Rejoice whatever anguish rend your heart
That God has given you a priceless dower
To live in these great times and have your part
In Freedom's crowning hour.

That you may tell your sons who see the light
High in the Heaven, their heritage to take:
'I saw the power of darkness put to flight,
I saw the morning break.'[1]

'The powers of darkness put to flight . . . the morning break.' Are those words really true as we'd like them to be? As true as we honestly believed them to be when for example, in our tent on that May evening in the Po valley in Italy, we learned that the war was over for us. . . .

We were stationed on the Yugoslav border in the hills near Trieste when I was asked to go by car to visit all the Eighth Army land-leave route camps from Italy to Calais. I was to visit every camp on the way up and coming back, and was allowed a certain freedom of route—in short and in army language, I was allowed to 'swan'.

Of course I took my driver with me, a young Londoner,

[1] Sir Owen Seaman: quoted by permission of the proprietors of *Punch*.

I

Driver George Colmer of the Kent Yeomanry, who was as faithful a fellow as one could hope to have and used to make remarks like 'Beggin' your pardon, sir, but it's an 'ell of a way'. Roy King came with me too as a spare driver but chiefly because he was such a good chap, and almost as an after-thought I took an older man who volunteered for the Navy, was accepted by the R.A.F., called up by the A.T.S. and landed in the Army!

I took Charlie Chislett because he is an expert photographer. But had I known him then as well as I got to know him I would have taken him in any case! He was a most cheerful fellow who had travelled a lot before the war and was full of good stories—I'll never forget how he told us once he was thrown over the side of a hill by a horse in Switzerland, the horse falling after him; and his wife when she saw him get up was so worried as she looked at him because she thought that the horse must have kicked him in the face—but it hadn't. He had always looked like that. Wives can be *so* tactless (they tell me).

I could have travelled to the end of the earth with these fellows. Even a dull journey—which this wasn't by a very long way—could have been cheerful with them. The people with whom we travel are so much more important than the place to which and through which we have to travel. I mean there are some people—we've not only met them—but sometimes *are* them ourselves—who can turn heaven to hell or perhaps even hell to heaven. The people we're with make all the difference. And sometimes we forget that—until it's too late: well Roy and Charlie and George will never let me forget it.

It was a wonderful journey from Trieste through Italy, Austria, Germany, Luxemburg, Belgium, and France. So we came to Calais, and before we turned back we saw the white cliffs of Dover. 'It's a glorious day to see them,' said the young British sailor who called me up to his

observation post. 'You couldn't get a better morning, sir.'
And as I looked on that bright early morning there they
were—there was 'Home!'

Home! The dream of countless thousands of men—many
who had never seen home for over four years. Home—
which because of their sacrifice and the sacrifice of those
they'd left behind them is *still* Home, thank God—still ours,
still British. As we drove back to Sedan, through the battle-
fields of the last war—and some of this—the words of a song
kept recurring. Sometimes someone would whistle it,
sometimes sing it out loud—almost unconsciously it seemed.
You all know it, it's a bit sentimental perhaps, but we're
none the worse of a bit of sentiment in the hard days:

> *There'll be blue birds over*
> *The white cliffs of Dover . . .*
> *There'll be joy and laughter*
> *And peace ever after.*

I wondered. . . . I wondered, would there be? Oh, it's
good to have our ideals, our dreams, our castles in the air;
but once we *have* our 'castles in the air' we need to build the
right foundations—the foundations of—yes, of 'joy and
laughter and peace ever after'.

I don't know whether it was the sight of the white cliffs
or the fact that he saw them on his twenty-first birthday, or
what it was, but George developed a temperature of 103
degrees and we had to leave him behind at Sedan (it's all
right, he came back again to Italy some days later!), and so
Roy took the wheel and drove us for nearly two thousand
miles—the rest of the journey; so you see, the precaution of
taking a spare driver was very necessary after all.

We returned through Belgium and Luxemburg and saw
again the battered cities—almost razed to the ground some
of them—of Germany and Austria: Mannheim, Mainz,
Munich. So did we see Dachau, the place of horror and

broken and battered lives. So did we see again when staying some days there with the 16/5 Lancers, Ulm with its glorious Gothic-towered Cathedral, standing almost untouched, with nothing but ruins around it. So back over the Danube—not a very blue Danube, I must confess—through lovely countryside and the words of the song returned:

> There'll be blue birds over
> The white cliffs of Dover . . .
> There'll be joy and laughter
> And peace ever after.

Somebody would whistle it again. And I wondered then, as I sometimes wonder now, would there be 'love and laughter and peace'? Not for some men—afraid to look the folk they love in the face; and not for some women either; and in Europe the countless refugees without homes, without fuel for fire, without sufficient food. I remembered the little French boy who shared our meal at the side of the road and told us that all they had to eat at home was *soupe et legumes*—soup and vegetables; and the German children at the side of the road who never begged, yet rushed to pick up yesterday's crusts.

> . . . . *joy and laughter*
> *And peace ever after.*

Was that just a 'castle in the air' or was it possible having rightly got it there to begin now to build the right foundation?

So on we went until we came to Berchtesgaten, and there we spent one night where the Americans gave us a most friendly reception and put us all up at one of the really good hotels there. It's one of the loveliest places in all the world surely is Berchtesgaten village—and yet, not far from it is the place where Hitler lived and dreamed his dreams—his castles in the air (and some very much on the earth), on the wrong foundations.

Most of Hitler's headquarters have been blasted—his house, Goering's house, the S.S. barracks and all the rest are examples of the extraordinary accuracy of the R.A.F. bombing. We went round Hitler's and Goering's house (neither, of course, was at home) and round the other places—a glorious sunny day and what lovely countryside!

High though Hitler's H.Q. stands—Roy had doubts as to whether the old car could make it, and even greater doubts as to how far the brakes would hold on the way down—high though it stands, we got into a jeep and climbed still higher—very high indeed: in fact, twice the height of the highest mountain in Britain—to Hitler's mountain 'hide-out'—the Eagle's Nest—an exceedingly high mountain from which he could look upon the world and imagine himself its master—an exceedingly high mountain where he dreamt of world power. Yes, and one does feel an amazing sensation of power when looking from the Eagle's Nest—the world in all its glory seems to stretch endlessly below.

Then suddenly the words came back to me—no, not the words of the 'White Cliffs of Dover' but the words of the 'Old Book': 'The devil taketh him unto an exceeding high mountain and showeth him all the kingdoms of the world, and the glory of them; and he said unto him, All these things will I give thee, if thou wilt fall down and worship me.' And Hitler from the exceedingly high mountain fell down and worshipped the Devil; and because the Devil is always a liar, Hitler, at the expense of great suffering to countless innocent folk, was beaten off the face of the earth.

Yet, as I looked from the exceeding high mountain, from the Eagle's Nest, I saw again that first picture—that picture of the only real Man who ever lived and who did not 'fall down'—the real story (d'you remember?)—'and he taketh him unto an exceeding high mountain and showeth him all the kingdoms of the world, and the glory of them; and he said unto him: All these things will I give thee, if thou wilt fall down and worship me.'

He, who alone has shown us what true manhood is, said: 'Get thee hence. . . . Thou shalt worship the Lord thy God, and him only shalt thou serve.' So the Lord of all Good Life went out as a conqueror—not of lands, nor of the kingdoms of the world—but of the hearts of men. The one true source of

Joy and laughter
And peace ever after

These then are the two pictures, and the white cliffs of Dover are linked with the heights of Berchtesgaten by the answer to the 'if'—all things 'if'. We all know what the things of the Devil are and there's no use pretending we don't—and to fall down to them and not to the things of God just means that there will be vultures over the white cliffs of Dover and endless misery and no real peace. Yes, we all know it—and that's the terrifying thing about it. 'What worries me,' said Mark Twain once, 'are not the bits of the Bible I don't understand, but the bits I do!'

It's so trite, but yet it needs to be said so often that if only we'd carry into the peace the service and the sacrifice that war demands, and realize that it means a cross, then we'll find the only way that leads to joy and laughter and real peace ever after both for ourselves and for those around us. We will have equated the white cliffs of Dover and the mountain of Berchtesgaten with 'The Green Hill far away outside the city wall'.

'It's a glorious day to see them,' said the young British sailor. 'You couldn't get a better morning.' A glorious morning—I wonder. The sailor said it was. The soldier saw it was. It's up to us to prove them right.

'There are glorious days ahead', said Sir James Barrie

Photo by Edward Moffatt, Edinburgh
'They say there's a ghost in my house'
Acheson House, Edinburgh

once, 'if you choose to make them glorious.' If we *choose*
—for only then can *we* really say what the sailor said and
the soldier saw.

> *I saw the powers of darkness put to flight,*
> *I saw the morning break.*

'You couldn't get a better morning'—IF.

Two

You Can't Take It With You: or the 'Casa Dusé'

They say there's a ghost in my house. I don't know
I've never seen him—and I used to sleep in the so-called
'haunted room'. Two of my friends—very reliable people
—claim to have seen him—a man with a large black
moustache, and a knife in his hand. I haven't lost a minute's
sleep over it. Though, frankly, unlike Shelley, I don't think
I should be overjoyed if I met him. You may remember
how Shelley the poet wrote:

> *While yet a boy I sought for ghosts, and sped*
> *Through many a listening chamber, cave and ruin,*
> *And starlight wood, with fearful steps pursuing*
> *Hopes of high talk with the departed dead.*

I don't think many of us pursue ghosts: we'd most of us
rather keep out of their way! . . . Do I believe in ghosts?
I neither believe nor disbelieve.

I remember that question, 'Do you believe in ghosts?'
being asked once at a Brains Trust—rather an extraordinary
Brains Trust it was too. It was held in a valley near Monte
Grande—some of you who were in Italy may remember.
The noise of gunfire was at times quite deafening, and the
enemy were very near—much too near, but life went on
almost as usual. We got used to the noise, we took for
granted the close proximity of the enemy; and a ghost with
a black moustache and a knife would have been a welcome
relief from those who were far from ghosts, whose weapons

were far more to the point than any knife. So we carried on our way—held concerts and services, and even talking-picture shows, debated, had lectures and Brains Trusts. The Royal Corps of Signals ran the Brains Trust at our Divisional Headquarters, and this then was the question that night, 'Does the Brains Trust believe in ghosts?' Well there were some fairly obvious observations, mostly in the negative, a couple of apocryphal ghost stories, and then one fellow said: 'I don't know about ghosts, but I do know this —and it may have something to do with it—I do know that some houses have a feeling about them—a good feeling or a bad feeling. You can often go into a house and feel that someone very nice or very nasty has lived there. I've often had that feeling,' he said. We all agreed. Some houses do often have a feeling about them; an aura which seems to have something to do with the folk who have lived there —or even live there now.

There is a wonderful passage in the memoirs of the Grand Duchess Marie of Russia, of her going back to her father's house after he had been brutally murdered by the Bolsheviks, with so many others she loved. For many years the house had stood unused; but as she went into all the rooms, the charm, the love of her father and his wife came back to her. She felt it all again in the atmosphere of the place. She didn't notice really its empty bareness, but lived again—was back in spirit again to the days she'd loved as a child.

That was the place she knew. But it can come too —this influence—this 'aura'—to places to which we've never been.

I felt it most strongly when I stayed once for a week in Asolo, near Treviso, in Italy. In this lovely ancient little town, where Robert Browning sometimes lived, and which he loved so much, I stayed in the Casa Dusé—a most charming house now belonging to the Earl of Iveagh. But it had belonged to Eleanora Dusé, one of the greatest actresses the world has ever known. She died in 1924, but 'the Great Dusé' is still a well-loved name.

She must have been, to the youth of Italy of our fathers' day, much what Ellen Terry was to the youth here. You remember how it was said that men used to propose to their girls in such words as these: 'As I can't get Ellen Terry, may I have you?' Well, Daniel Varé tells how Eleanora Dusé was to the youth of Italy, 'the symbol of all the beauty and the loving in the world'—what a lovely phrase that is—what a wonderful description of someone—'the symbol of all the beauty and the loving in the world'! Was it not of her that her lover Gabriele d'Annunzio (who loved her more and in a different way than she loved him), wrote: 'Ella cantava: e il puro canto rendara pure tutte le cose'—which any person who has been in Italy can translate—'She sang, and her pure song made all things seem pure'—(would that more songs and singers were like that!). 'The symbol of all the beauty and the loving in the world.' And you felt it in that house, you know, set in the lovely surroundings; there was a loveliness and beauty around you, and you felt that though you had never met her, she was there.

One day as I sat in the garden, on a lovely Italian evening looking on to the emerald plains with the hills beyond—a part of the Alps—grapes hanging from the vines, and the birds singing, there came from some house near, across the stillness—as if to crown it all—the clear notes of a piano, that glorious Second Movement of Beethoven's 'Pathetique': he left that—and much else—to the world.

What are we leaving? and what influence do we have here and now on people? For every one of us in some way influences others for good or ill. What haunting memories do we sometimes have of how we might have been kinder to him—or to her—and now it all *seems* too late.

In what I feel is one of the most moving passages in modern literature, Hugh Walpole describes the misery of

Mr. Perrin, who had tried to do his best in his love for Gardiner Minimus, and how the constant rejection of all his care for the boy had been spurned, driving Mr. Perrin to suicide as he threw himself over a cliff. Later Gardiner, walking along the cliff, but not knowing the fate of the man who had done so much to help him, paused and looked out to sea above the cove. 'Perrin,' he said to himself, 'although a bit of an ass, was a good sort' . . . he would behave more decently next term; he would make up a bit; he was a queer beggar, Perrin, but he meant to be decent to him . . . next term.

But 'next term' never came, and there are quite a lot of folk who know just what that means.

I remember too, Dick Sheppard telling once how he could 'never forget looking in the face of his father when life had left the dear body, and thinking of the times unnumbered when I had failed to tell him what I owed to him. They tell me,' he said, 'that when I was young, he and my mother went without things to give me of the best. I know that the thoughts of his last years were centred around me. I wonder now if there is an angel who can take him a message that will tell him that, as all the years go by, I am increasingly grateful to him. On the last Sunday of his life he expected me to have supper with him, and told my mother several times, he was certain I should come. I was tired, and didn't go. This is a thing that haunts me now it is too late.'

Well, 'Dear Dick'—as people loved to call him—has gone now too, and what a wonderful legacy he left behind!

What are we leaving behind? What influence have we *now*? Equally important, what sort of people are we allowing to influence us?

Oh, I know we can't always choose that very easily. We can't choose the people in our work or our street or our club. We are glad of some, accept others, and have to put up with the rest.

But most people have some leisure time too—and our influence (and character) is more dependent on our leisure hours really than our working hours—that's to say if we are really working—and usually a man can choose the influences of his leisure hours, and no one dare trifle with that. As my friend Mr. George Troup has said: 'If you trifle with your leisure you trifle with your life.'

So it's not only a good thing, but a right thing, to belong to a society of people who are honestly making an effort to be influenced by the highest power we know—the power of God, and that's one of the reasons, of course, why there's the Church. The Church isn't just a hothouse for weak-kneed people or the 'precious' or the 'unco' guid.' The Church is much more a hospital for middling and great sinners who need mending, at least (*at least*) once a week.

People don't go to Church because they're better than other folk—or shouldn't. They go, first, and right at the beginning of the Service, to ask forgiveness for all they've done wrong.

The old word is 'sin', but people don't like that word nowadays: it makes them feel uncomfortable and sounds almost indecent.

Oh, I know that some of you think that a lot of people who go to Church are hypocrites. You're quite right. In some form or another I suppose we're all hypocrites. But be very careful whom you regard as a hypocrite (apart from yourself). Sometimes a hypocrite is just an ordinary fellow who's trying his best, and in spite of his effort failing more often than he cares to admit, and that's far better than a man who doesn't try at all—or who tries to think he's all right —and knows he isn't.

The point I want to make is that those who belong to (and so go to) a church, are seeking an influence which is far more than an influence, a fellowship which is no ordinary fellowship, and who are honestly making an effort to 'see life steadily and see it whole'; they are, in short, making an honest effort to influence those around them and quite literally, 'for the good of their souls'.

Then too, we must *allow* ourselves to be influenced by men really greater, and so better, than ourselves. There's a tendency nowadays—especially among younger people—to think that 'everyone's as good as everyone else'—an appalling bit of conceit. We must cultivate the right sort of friendships, whether in life or in books.

We must never forget the greatest of all libraries, which is in everyone's power to possess—the Book we call the Bible. It's not a dull book if you read it with intelligence, though sometimes, I admit, it's rather dully 'got up'. It's not an ordinary book; but it's written by ordinary men who were inspired to write it—inspired, we believe, by God Himself to write it, and so it contains for us the Word of God. That is, God speaks to us in and through the Bible, as in no other book, and that is what helps make the Bible like no other book—or collection of books of history, drama, essays, songs, poetry, biography and autobiography, for that's what it really is.

Seek then the influence not only of the Church, but of the Bible. And lastly, seek direct influence from God Himself, in what we call prayer, about which I've spoken to you so often before. All the really great men I've known have 'faced their Maker', as my old Colonel once put it to me, in the morning and at night.

It's really all far more simple than we try to make out—this business of living and influencing and being influenced. Put yourself in the hands of God, work hard, do what you can for your fellows, and be perfectly natural, which means having a sense of humour—one of God's greatest gifts to mankind.

My friend Geoffrey Gilbey reminded me the other day, when I was staying with him in Chelsea, of a definition once given of a successful life, and it ran something like this: 'He has achieved success who has lived well, laughed often, and loved much; who has gained the respect of intelligent men, and the love of little children; who has filled his niche and accomplished his task; who has left the world better than he found it, whether by an improved garden, a perfect poem, or a rescued soul; who has never lacked appreciation of earth's beauty, or failed to express it; who has always looked for the best in others and given the best he had; whose life was an inspiration; whose memory a benediction.'

So I leave you tonight with two questions.

What sort of influence are you now? What will people remember you best by when you die? And perhaps one other—which matters most—*Will they be right?*

Three

'NOT A HEALTHY SORT OF PARTY, SIR'

I spent two nights and a day recently in that place I love so much—the Yarrow Valley. It's a glorious place is the Yarrow Valley, with its clean, searing gales and friendly green hills stretching like gentle waves as far as the eye can see. But if you don't know the Yarrow Valley, perhaps you can console yourself by remembering with Wordsworth:

> *Enough if in our hearts we know*
> *There's such a place as Yarrow.*

I had with me two fellows from my church who were on leave—Stanley McLean in the Scots Guards, and Tommy McLean in the Royal Navy, and we stayed where I sometimes stay, in the little inn where for the last time Sir Walter Scott and the Ettrick Shepherd met.

The weather was—shall we say seasonable for January?— freezing cold one day and lashing with rain the next. But Stanley and Tommy are the kind of companions I like—the 'never mind the weather, never mind the rain' type, who'll go out for a walk in any weather, who love the fresh air and the wind in your face and the sting of the rain—grim at first, decidedly uncomfortable, but in the words of Thomas Hardy, 'A hardship to be calendared'. But what a wonderful feeling one gets afterwards—'fitness'—that's the word—a rub down with a rough towel till your face tingles with a shining warmth, then a chair at the fire, a book, a pipe—what a lot folk miss who don't get out in the wind and the rain. 'There's the wind on the heath, brother; if I could only feel that I would gladly live for ever,' said Jasper. So Robert Louis Stevenson in the stuffy heat of the tropics remembering to the end his well-loved places could write to S. R. Crockett: 'Blows the wind on the moors today and the sun and the rain are flying, Blows the wind on the moors today?' And the old Scottish proverb becomes more telling! 'Ye maun tak' the wind in your face, gin we would meet wi' God.' Oh yes, what a lot people miss, whose only entertainment is the picture-house or the dance hall, billiards, or the club, and who feel with Hazlitt's Sir Flopling Flutter that 'beyond Hyde Park is all a desert'.

So I thought and felt again as with sweaters and shorts these two companions walked with me in the wind and the rain over Walter Scott's best-loved valley and that of the Ettrick Shepherd.

The last time I walked with Stanley had been before the war. At the age of eighteen he had gone out with the Scots Guards to Egypt and seen service there and in Eritrea, in Syria, and in Palestine, and with the Western Desert Force and the Eighth Army in Africa and Italy. And Tommy— well, Tommy was eleven years old when I left Edinburgh with the Dandy Ninth in 1939. That was well over six years ago and now he's in the Navy. I thought again as I often think of the fellows who used to walk with us, but who won't walk with us again. Jimmie and Jackie, Jim Stewart, Willie Brown, Jim Stobie, David Adams, and all the others. What a lot extra we've got to put into life now, to make up for their loss.

Though the old firm remains so much the same these years have brought great changes. I admit that the changes are on both sides; for we who have just come out of the Army miss the wonderful fellowship, the sharing of common dangers and pleasures, the brewing up of tea at the roadside, the quite spontaneous desire to work with and for each other. But there's a change on the other side too. People out for themselves again, bad manners, even downright rudeness at times. Oh, I know quite well the excuses, but whatever the excuse is and however understandable bad manners remain bad manners, and rudeness remains rudeness. Yes, whatever the excuse is; and it's all so unfriendly really, and so unnecessary.

After all, we in Scotland have least excuse of all for it. True you've had your share of worry and sadness, and some have had a grim and heavy burden to bear, and people, I know, can suffer and worry far more for folk than the folk worry and suffer for themselves. But all your hardships and sufferings have been one with practically the whole world, who in addition—*in addition*—have had to bear such things as folk here have only read. True you had a bit of bombing here, a few very bad nights on Clydeside, raids on north-east Scotland, but that was not compared to the London blitz of 1940, or the eighty days of the flying bombs, and rockets. Our country was not occupied by enemy troops, we've always had something to eat and wear. Oh yes, we ought to be very thankful, very thankful indeed—and I know that very many are and show it. But sometimes one wonders, and has a very good reason to wonder.

Or take our attitude to religion. Crowded churches on days of National Prayer, and to be fair, on great days of thanksgiving, 'Praise God from whom all blessings flow'—and all the rest of it.

But what now? Hopeless indifference—no, no, not antagonism, but indifference. I suppose folk think that now that the war is over, it doesn't matter so much. You've got what you want from the Father, and so you can go on your way again. 'He's a decent Chap,' you say, 'and we can always go back to Him again.' In any case the war may be won, but the peace isn't, and one can't help being reminded sometimes of the story of the old lady who said to the great Duke of Wellington: 'What a great thing, sir, a victory must be.' To which the Iron Duke replied: 'It's the next greatest disaster, madam, to a defeat.'

Well, I suppose you agree with all that, but say: 'I know, but what on earth can I do about it?' Or, 'Isn't this the job of the United Nations, the Government, the T.U.C., UNRRA, and so on?' But as a matter of fact unless *you* do something about it, none of these organizations can really do much at all.

Now I wonder how many of you have read *Beyond the Chindwin*. It's Colonel Bernard Ferguson's book of the Wingate Expedition of 1943 to Burma, and it's just grand reading. It's a story supremely well worth telling, and surely there is no one who could have told it better than Bernard Ferguson who at the time, a Major in the Black Watch, led No. 5 Column. The feats of endurance, the humour, the expert planning, the grim realities, the best type of discipline, the moments of excited suspense. Oh yes, it's a grand book. And in it you read of people you would dearly love to meet (or in some cases, alas, to have met), even if it were just to shake them by the hand. (I once met a young corporal in the Signals, who told me that he'd felt a different man since Field-Marshal Alexander had shaken him by the hand.) Most of the men in this book were so-called ordinary fellows too—civilians in uniform, not specially picked, many in fact, second-line troops. As I've hinted, some of them won't come back, some of the best, like that young Rhodes Scholar in the Black Watch, Duncan Menzies. He was captured and tied to a tree by the Japanese, and then brutally killed by them. There was the time, for instance, when starving, tired, and exhausted with heat by day, frozen with cold at night, pestered with flies and mosquitoes, and a long way still to go, he could yet turn to his Column Commander and say: 'Well this may be hell, but I wouldn't have missed even this part of the trip.' (This is reminiscent of Captain Scott of the Antarctic, who in a similar position said: 'How much better is all this than sitting in too great comfort at home.') As Bernard Ferguson continued his sad way without Duncan Menzies, the words of Walter Scott came back to him:

> He is gone on the mountain,
> He is lost to the forest,
> Like a summer-dried fountain,
> When our need was the sorest.
> The fount, reappearing,
> From the raindrops shall borrow,
> But to us comes no cheering,
> To Duncan no morrow!

Such men, thank God, there still are. Men who can still balance the far-too-heavily weighted scale of those who seek in life the easy and so-called comfortable way, and for enjoyment the things they can buy; and grouse, and feel flat, and usually blame someone else when things don't turn out quite as they want. Yes, the men in this story, give us a refreshingly different picture, so that with Field-Marshal Lord Wavell we can say: 'May the spirit of adventure and self-sacrifice be rekindled and stay with us after the war, when we undertake the greatest adventure yet made on the human race to refashion a shattered world.'

But the one man who for me stands out above all the others in this grand book is hardly mentioned at all. He was a young sergeant. Yes, here too we must use the past tense, who though setting out as a lance-corporal was soon promoted. His name is Lance-Sergeant Gunn—and the reason why he stands out above all the others?

Cut off as some were from his original column he later attached himself to some troops who were also seeking their way back to India. Not long after, Bernard Ferguson's column met him, this time leading a small party of his own, most of them men older than himself. What was he doing, and how had he got there? 'This lad, who can't have been more than twenty-two, and was younger than most of the men he was commanding and over whom he had so much influence'—how had he got there? Well, the troops he'd joined up with, he didn't feel were 'A healthy sort of party, sir, not according to my idea'. So he'd broken away from them and become his own leader, though at great risk, in the way he knew to be healthier, and found as always that there were some ready to follow. 'Here,' writes Colonel Ferguson, 'was the chap who realized that a few stout hearts would fare better by themselves than among a number who showed signs of going craven.' A few stout hearts will fare better by themselves. How true that is of all life, and that's what you and I can do about it. And it's as true in civilian life as in the Navy, Army or the Air Force.

Of course, it's not always possible to do what Sergeant Gunn was able to do, and actually break right off. But it is always possible for a fellow however young, to go the way he knows to be the healthy way; and it's equally possible for those who are—well, just not quite leaders—to find such a chap (never mind if he's younger) to follow.

You and I have met both sorts in the Army and out of it. The few stout hearts who in striking out on their own, and refusing to be led off and influenced by things that are not —well—are not healthy, always fare better and in the long run far more cheerfully than the craven heart.

It requires such men as Sergeant Gunn and his kind to make us realize again what Mr. Churchill's doctor, Lord Moran, has recently written: 'All the fine things in war, as in peace, are the work of a few men, the honour of our race is in the keeping of but a fraction of her people.' Yet the pity is that it should be the few and not the many. For only when the few become the many or at least can sufficiently lead or influence the many can lasting peace be found, whether in the hearts of men or in the world in which men live.

After all, one leader with eleven followers nearly two thousand years ago—but that's another story.

Or is it?

Four

THE FIRST ELEVEN

The life of a parson—whether he be a padre or a parish minister—can (and I think really should be) one of the most varied in the world. There are some people who think we are all very 'green'—a cross between a prep. schoolboy and a Victorian spinster (though incidentally they both know a great deal more than they are given credit for!) Of course, that's frightful nonsense. There's not much we don't know by the very nature of our work. We are constantly being brought into all sorts of situations from every different angle. Our range has to be wide—we've got to be cheerful at a wedding and serious at a funeral; we've got to discuss Gordon Smith's football on the same afternoon, perhaps, as the latest book on theology or philosophy. So as well as reading the *Spectator* or *The New Statesman* and *The Times*, we follow the fortunes or misfortunes of the Broons, listen to Geraldo, and discuss the pros and cons of nationalization.

Oh yes! A life full of interest and interests—meeting all sorts of folk and listening to all sorts of stories in many different places—'all things to all men' yet but with one common purpose behind it if we are to be true to our vocation—the making of God real to men; and this means a very strict disciplining of ourselves—from which, speaking for myself, I too often fail.

But I'm not going to discuss the parson's life—though sometimes I feel it wouldn't be a bad thing to do if for no

Danie Fourie at Lake Como

other reason than to clear up some misunderstandings.

'All sorts of folk, all sorts of stories in many different places.' So it was that one night last summer while having dinner in a mess-tent on the Yugoslav border, I heard this story from the colonel of a famous Indian Regiment.

Our conversation had ranged rather trivially all over the place, and then I mentioned a famous regiment (I don't think that's giving anything away for what regiment now *isn't* a famous one?) One of this regiment's regular battalions had been nearly wiped out in the Far East in the early days of the war.

'Did you ever hear', said the Colonel, 'the story as to how some of them got away?' I told him I hadn't. 'Well,' he said, 'it's a most interesting story and I have it from one of the men himself.' Then he told me how this great and gallant battalion had fought its way most brilliantly, contesting every mile of ground till now there were only about two hundred left, and the position was really quite hopeless. But there were still some aircraft—enough to take about seventy men—and the Colonel was determined to get as many as possible out—to save as many good lives as possible —to let the battalion's fate be known and to show others how best to profit from the lessons they had learned. Two hundred left and seventy to be chosen. How was he going to do it? How would you have done it? Well, this is what he did, and I think you will agree it was a very good way— in fact, the best way possible.

He got the men round him and told them quite simply and bluntly that the position was desperate, that they had all fought as he'd known from the beginning they would, brilliantly and bravely, and now he called on them to do one thing more. He wanted about seventy men to volunteer for a suicide job—a job that might mean certain death. It was a lot to ask, he confessed, but he had no doubt that he would get them. Well, he got them all right, and chose the

C

first seventy volunteers; and so, they who were willing to lose their lives for the sake of their comrades and their country found they had gone to almost certain life. Risking all, their very lives in the service of their fellow men (and may it be said in the service of God!), willing to lose life itself, they found it.

Yes, that's the text, you've got it—'Whoever is willing to lose his life for My sake will find it.'

That brings me back to the eleven men I mentioned at the end of the last chapter, these men we call the Apostles; and I'd like to put out of your head any preconceived ideas you may have about them. For some strange reason, most people regard them as men—barely men—with long beards and haloes round their heads and more or less fossilized in stained-glass windows. It's extraordinary how people get certain ideas and won't budge from them.

When I was rather short of literature once in Italy, I picked up a book on the life of the flea. My ideas about the flea were preconceived and I'm happy to say scarcely based on personal experience; and I found an extraordinary lot about the flea that I'd never dreamt about before. For example, that there are over six hundred different kinds of fleas, and monkeys are far less liable to have fleas than human beings. In fact, monkeys don't have fleas, they acquire them from us. Our fleas are called *pulex irritans*, which seems very suggestive—and so on.

What's that? What has this got to do with the Apostles? Nothing of course, directly, but the point is that people get preconceived ideas and have sometimes to be shaken out of them—whether they are ideas about fleas or Apostles, and as I've said we've got the Apostles all wrong, for they were just ordinary men, doing ordinary jobs, no two alike, indeed all very different—that's what they were; although they became different. What really made them become different was that they were willing to lose their own lives in order to find real life—yes, quite literally, they were willing to throw everything up and start again. That's important, and I notice that Mr. C. S. Lewis stresses that point in the introduction to *The Great Divorce*. 'A wrong sum can be put right, but only by going back till you find the error and working it from that point. Never by simply going on.' Evil can be undone, but it cannot develop into good.

So what those eleven men did was just to go back to the start where they'd gone off the road, and having got there, go ten times quicker along the new road to make up for lost time, and in the hands of the Father, these ordinary men saw that the secret was to become as children in order to grow into men, real men. They took their Young Leader completely at His word. In Him they saw man as he should be and He their Leader, saw in them—as He sees in all men—men as they could be. 'The task of leadership is not to put greatness into humanity, but to elicit it, for the greatness is already there,' said John Buchan once, when speaking to the St. Andrews students on the great Montrose. And that's what happened to these eleven ordinary men. The Lord of all good life brought out the greatness in them: 'Ye are the Light of the world', He said—and they became the light of the world.

'Ye are the Light of the world', and He said it to— well, a hard-boiled business man called Matthew, an impetuous fisherman called Simon (whom knowing his potential weakness and potential greatness, he nicknamed Petros, the Greek word for a rock); a fiery Nationalist called Simon too—Simon the Zealot—always 'agin the Government'; a canny fellow, a bit of a Scot, called Thomas; a young fellow called John, who must have been a bit of a handful at times in his early days, for he and his brother were called the 'sons of thunder'. And so on. 'Ye are the Light of the world'—and sure enough they became the light of the world. No, no, not stained-glass saints (in actual fact most of the saints have had more courage in their little finger than most men have in their whole body!), but as men who had gone back to where they'd gone off the road, and started off again with a firmer step—and sometimes on their knees.

All through their lives, they still had difficulties to overcome. The business man, St. Matthew, constantly would have the memory of his past before him—yet he went on in this new-found way, and tradition tells us he was the first missionary in Ethiopia. St. Peter, the fisherman, still found his impetuosity getting the better of him, still found it hard at times to stand up against public opinion, still lost his temper—and no doubt his language at times was a bit basic —but he went on the way and was crucified in Rome—no coward at the end, but with a blessing, not a curse on his lips. St. Thomas, who found it hard to believe anything unless he saw it in writing or with his eyes, and yet who had the sense to remain in the fellowship, though he couldn't quite believe everything they told him, St. Thomas, the protagonist of the 'common sense' view of life, well, he kept on the way and died a martyr's death near Madras, where you can still see the little mound of St. Thomas. Or St. Andrew, the first missionary overshadowed by his more forceful brother, St. Peter—Andrew never could quite see the difficulty and got on pretty well with everybody in a light-hearted fashion, but he kept to the way, and tradition tells that he preached to the Russians, and that is why he is the patron saint of Russia. Later he went to Greece, and in trying to persuade the pro-consul's wife to make a public announcement of her conversion to Christianity—he didn't see any difficulty in this as in anything else: however, other people did and he was crucified on a cross whose shape is so well known to Scotsmen as it now forms our National flag and the divisional badge of the Lowland Division.

So with them all, though not all were martyred on the

way. Tough young John became the old Bishop of Ephesus, for example. Though Herod's sword had divided the Sons of Thunder, and St. James 'knew in what sense the Father had chosen him to be first among the Apostles'. Of St. John's death we know nothing, but tradition tells of him as an old, old man being lifted on the shoulders of the presbyters, saying with an old man's whisper: 'My little children, love one another.'

So these eleven men, all so different, went on the new way, the Way of their Leader. 'I am the Way,' he had said to them.

It must have been an amazing sight really to see a man of the 'left' and a man of the 'right'—a business man and a politician—a timid man, a strong rough fisherman—going cheerfully on the same way. 'And one day', said their Leader, 'when I am lifted up, I will draw all men to me, all ordinary men like you into one brotherhood, one day all men will be men of the Way.'

But—what's that you say, 'Haven't you left one out? Weren't there twelve?' Of course there were, and I have left him out because he didn't go back and start again—he deserted and met a terrible end, committed suicide you remember. Yes, I left him out, you were quite right.

But there was one later on whom I feel I should mention, for he fits in no uncertain way into what I've been saying. He was like a lot of present-day men too. He thought the Christian faith was dangerous and not at all sound. He was rather a learned man and 'knew what he was talking about'—in fact, the whole thing ought to be stamped out and put down, and he did his level best to do this. He joined in the pogrom, and amongst those he helped to kill was a young man called Stephen, But he came out all right in the end, and became the greatest of them all really; in fact he too was martyred after some time in concentration camp and prison. Yes, there was even a chance for Saul of Tarsus, and he took it—and the Central Cathedral of the British Commonwealth and Empire, the Cathedral which stood through all the blitzes of the enemy, is called after him.

As Oscar Wilde once said: 'The Saint is someone with a past, the sinner with a future.'

This then is the story of some ordinary men like you and me, who found the secret of life and showed how all men of all nations, however different their views or their temperaments are, can be united if we but follow them. And if we but follow them, we'll find that ahead of us goes the Leader they followed.

Five

THE RELIGION OF THE MOUNTAIN

Once, as I may have told you before, while I was sitting in an East Lothian inn, I was talking to one of our most famous Scottish artists. He was getting on in years, but still his old skill remained, his enthusiasm, his love of simple things and lovely things. We talked a bit, and then he said to me: 'I don't know, padre, what your idea of heaven is like. For myself I don't think it could be more lovely than the world we live in. Look,' he said, 'look at that sunset yonder: could anything be more—yes, "heavenly"'—he smiled a bit then—'more heavenly than that?' I replied: 'It's good to hear you say that, sir; yes, the sunset *is* lovely and there are some lovely things, but there are many many things that are more hellish than heavenly. With all the wonderful courage and love and friendship of people, there's so much that's bad in us all: children with few chances, jealousy, brutality, dirtiness—and I needn't elaborate—no, sir, not at all like my idea of heaven I'm afraid.' Then the old artist looked up at me and said: 'I suppose the difference is that as an artist all my years I've looked for lovely things . . . and I've always found them.'

Well, we're not all artists—nor are all artists like him; but that day he taught me a wonderful lesson. Amid all life's sordidness there is still beauty to be found for those that seek it with the right heart, for few there are, I hope, like Soames Forsyte, who 'might wish and wish and never get it—the beauty and loving in the world'.

But while it isn't necessary to go outside your own country—or even county—to see beauty in the world of nature (after all what can be more glorious than looking out and seeing the glory of the sky?), it does add tremendously to the broad picture and deeper appreciation to see the other places. Most fellows of seventeen spend in a year as much in cigarettes and picture-houses and dances as could have taken them a conducted tour of the Mediterranean countries in the days before the last war.

For example, I shall never forget the wonder and amazement—the awe really—when I first saw certain parts of the Dolomites and the Tyrol: nor can I ever forget the views from my window of Lake Como from Catannabbia, or of Mount Zion from the Scottish Hospice in Jerusalem. But perhaps the most wonderful view I have ever seen was in Switzerland one glorious summer evening. We had come up from Italy through the great Simplon Pass where we saw, as Wordsworth saw: 'The immeasurable height of woods decaying never to be decayed'. We travelled the north-west corner of Lake Geneva and saw the castle of Chillon and the beautiful town of Lausanne. Then, about an hour's journey out, I saw the panorama of the Alps—the pink, snow-clad Vassal mountains stretching for over a hundred miles, and it seemed to infinity, with Mount Blanc, the king of them all, and the Dents de Midi and the Matterhorn as very royal princes.

What a wonderful sight it was and what a wonderful evening to see it! and I thought of the gallant band of men —the mountaineers who loved the high places and the adventures and hardships that lead them to them. I remembered how my friend Padre Jimmie Wood had put it once: 'I don't know how you feel about mountains and hill-climbing but I'm never happier than when I'm standing on some high windy ridge alone or with a companion in sunlight or in starlight far above the tree line and beyond the way of the golden plover. In such places I find a peace the world can never give.'

But it was the Matterhorn that thrilled me most—not so much the sight of it—though that, especially if you see it from the Italian side with its grand terrace walls and stretching for nearly fifteen thousand feet up, is thrill enough—but more the story of the men who had fought for its height and who had 'battered with fate and won through', and especially of a July day in 1865 when after seven attempts—that's what I like about these people—it was finally conquered by a party led by Edward Whymper. A great story it is—how they strove to the top, their wild boyish excitement when they got there, saw on that perfectly clear day all the well-kent mountains round, up to a hundred miles away or more, 'pleasant thoughts of happy days in bygone years came up unbidden as we recognized the old familiar forms. All were revealed, not one of the principal peaks of the Alps was hidden, we remained on the summit for an hour,' he said. 'One crowded hour of glorious life' passed away too quickly and they began to prepare for the descent.

All you who know about mountains will know what followed next—the horror and the tragedy of it all. . . . Not long after the descent began a 'sharp-eyed lad' ran into the Monte Rosa Hotel saying he had seen an avalanche fall from the summit of the Matterhorn. They told him in the hotel not to be silly; but he wasn't so silly after all. It was no avalanche certainly, but to the boy it might well have looked like one. What happened was roughly this. One of the party slipped, banged into another and knocked him over, the two fell downward and immediately the others with him—one of whom was Lord Francis Douglas. Edward Whymper and an old guide at the back held for all they were worth, but the rope broke below them and they saw their friends sliding over the banks spreading their hands in a vain effort to save themselves. 'They passed', said

Whymper, 'from our sight, disappeared one by one and fell from precipice to precipice—a distance of nearly four thousand feet: from the moment the rope broke, it was impossible to help them.'

For at least half an hour, Whymper and the two guides were terrified to move. A laughing cheerful party of but a few minutes before—and now only Whymper left with old Peter and young Peter—two guides—both quite paralysed with fear.

Fear! Oh yes, many of us know what cold fear can be like—real physical fear, and many folk too know the meaning of another sort of fear—fear of being found out, fear of being caught, fear of the future in life and after death.

Mark Hellinger, in one of his remarkable short stories, tells about a man whose one great fear was that he was going blind. His doctor told him it was possible, unless he was very careful; and this fear haunted him so much that he left his wife and family and took a small hut in the hills where he lived alone. At night he kept the cabin lights burning even when he was asleep and would wake up throughout the night in terror, open his eyes, see the light, and go to sleep again. From time to time, his friends would come to visit him, and one night a friend called and stayed unusually late, playing on a checker board. It was past midnight when the friend left, and having won ten out of twelve games, he was in good form, and just going off to bed, he said.

Next morning they heard that he was dead. He'd shot himself, and the postman had found him. They found a note to say that when his hour of darkness came on him, he would shoot himself. His friend of the night before rode back with the coroner. 'By the way,' he said, 'remind me to stop off at the power plant, will you? That storm last night blew out every light in Jenkins' cabin.' That's what fear did to him, and as in his case, the fear was groundless, so is most fear; I might almost say all fear. You'll probably read this somewhere: 'Today is the tomorrow we worried about yesterday.' Yes, worry is a form of fear. The commonest of all forms of fear, but 'Don't be afraid,' said our Lord, 'your heavenly Father knows and to the man and woman who is truly sorry, who really is trying, not all the world does can ever undo that love'. You may remember what an utter funk St. Peter was when that Thursday night a girl said to him: 'You're a follower of Jesus, aren't you?' And he said, of course he wasn't; and he said it more than once too. Then at the start of a new day the cock crew and he saw what a coward he had been and he wept bitterly— and it takes real sorrow to make a tough man weep. When our Blessed Lord came back again, He said, you remember: 'Go and tell the disciples, and don't forget to tell Peter.' You see, He was ready to start off fresh in the morning, and He's always ready; and St. Peter saw how groundless fear was and did the bravest thing a man could ever do—was martyred for his courage.

And there was paralysed fear on the Matterhorn that July day, but they got down all right; a strange descent it was, for as they slowly, sadly, went down the slope, they saw a great arch appear in the sky, 'pale, colourless, and noiseless, but perfectly sharp and defined, except when it was lost in the clouds. This unearthly apparition,' said Edward Whymper, 'it seemed like a vision from another world, and almost appalled, we watched with amazement the gradual development of two vast crosses, one on either side.' They all three saw it clearly. 'The spectral forms remained motionless; it was a fearful and wonderful sight and impressive beyond description coming at such a moment.' And later they found the bodies and left them where they fell, 'buried in snow at the base of the grandest cliff of the most majestic mountain in the Alps'. Then they found the cause of it all. There was but one weak link between old Peter who survived and Lord Francis Douglas who was killed, a weaker rope had been used, and this one small link had been the cause of changing life to death, joy to sadness, conquest to defeat. One small link made all the difference, one small link. How often that happens, and that small link can be even at times as small as you and I. Yes, even as small as that. 'For the loss of a nail, the shoe was lost', and that lost the battle in the end, remember. For want of a kind word in the right place, a woman's happiness was lost. For a minute's loss of control, a life was destroyed, joy turned to sadness. We have all different functions in the world and one man can throw the whole thing out of gear. And the Church—the greatest fellowship in the world—depends on the co-operation of every member in it. We are not all the same, but we all need each other. I'd like you to read the twelfth chapter of the first Epistle to the Corinthians. Here, for example, are some words from it in a modern translation: 'One man may evidence one kind of gift or service, one man's sphere of usefulness or inspiration may differ entirely from another's, but he will not differ in the spirit.' And then the great apostle tells us how the Church is the body of Christ in the world. 'The Church is as it were, one infinite body, wherein all the parts and members are mutually helpful and independent . . . hand cannot say to foot, "I have no need of you" . . . every part is beautifully formed to assist and be complementary to the other'—and here's the important bit—'If one member suffer, all suffer with it, and no one part of the body can be affected for good or ill, without the others feeling it.'

Yes, I'd like each one of ourselves to challenge ourselves again now and ask how we are affected in the whole. Is the bit that is you keeping folk in the path however difficult—or ready to hurl them to destruction? Is perhaps the reason why things are not going quite as well as they might due to some flaw somewhere and could that flaw possibly be you, I wonder, or me?

An awful thought, isn't it, but worth the thinking for a moment.

And what I like so much is that in spite of the disaster, Edward Whymper didn't stop climbing but went on; that others were not put off with the tragedy, but set out to conquer the Matterhorn with a determination and a spirit that was never more needed than in the present days—the same spirit, the same courage, the same vision in our ordinary ways that these men showed when they face mountains—climbing, adventuring, risking all to conquer, yes, that's what we need. 'Give me this mountain' said old Caleb in the Book of Joshua, a favourite text of my friend Tom Curr. 'We must expect', says the great scientist, Dr. A. M. Whitehead, 'that the future will disclose dangers. It is the business of the future to be dangerous.' Man as he really is, man at his best, is man when he is living dangerously, leaving the comfort of the plains, the ease of the shelter, and venturing out and up. This doesn't mean living foolishly of course, but it means, well, perhaps Browning puts it best: 'That lowman seeks a little thing to do, sees it and does it, that highman with a great thing to pursue dies e'er he knows it.' It means the spirit that made Whymper go on again, Shackleton set out after a former failure with 'Never for me the lost endeavour, never the lowered banner'—the Lord of life setting out for Jerusalem with steadfast face. Yes, that's what it means and that is man as he really is at his best.

The author of that great little book, *Arnhem Lift*, has brought this home to me again recently in a most dramatic and emphatic way. He tells us at the end of the thrilling Arnhem story how the life they led during those days in German-occupied Holland came nearer to a 'natural' existence than anything that could have been conceived, and yet how the more savage the fighting got, the more civilized the men seemed to become. 'By civilized,' he wrote, 'I don't mean having baths and being clean and shaving and eating with a knife and fork, but the relations between man and man; they became increasingly more polite and helpful, there was such a gentleness and friendship among them as would have made any of them almost uncomfortable back at the station.' Although they were fighting like tigers and in that fight had to be completely ruthless there was no tough behaviour or coarseness of speech. It was almost uncanny. All familiar army swear words and idioms were absent from their conversation, probably for the first time since any of them joined the Service. They were courteous kind, and considerate without any self-consciousness—man living dangerously, tackling heavy jobs. That is what I mean when to borrow a phrase of Field-Marshal Smuts, I talk of the 'religion of the mountain'. With these other thoughts there too came back to me as I gazed at the Matterhorn and the stretching Alps a speech that he once made on Table Mountain and these words of it: 'If we wish to express great intellectual or moral or spiritual attainment we use the language of altitudes. We speak of men who have risen, of aims and ideas that are lofty, we place the seat of our highest religious ideas in high heaven, and we consign all that is morally base to the nethermost hell . . . the mountain . . . has a great historic and spiritual meaning for us. It stands for us as the ladder of Life. Nay, more, it is the ladder of the soul, and in a curious way, the source of religion. From it came the Law, from it came the Gospel in the Sermon on the Mount. We may truly say that the highest religion is the religion of the mountain.'

The old artist then was surely right, not only about the world in which men live, but also about the world of men. If we look for the best in man, we'll find it, and find it in those whose religion is the religion of the mountain. The men who are without self-consciousness, because there's a bigger job to do. Life like that for any man meant 'going

strong for the top'. But as he went the view became more
lovely, the air became more clear, there was a deeper peace:

> *And all that he approved was sung,*
> *And most of what he saw was good.*

among bosom top, that is the word that was to become those slowly, his private name from that, therefore a long prayer and

that all that weakness and supply
but most a helper must not stay good.

Six

TWO CONQUERORS—WITH A DIFFERENCE

I've mentioned to you before some of the really first-class books that the late war has produced—like *Beyond the Chindwin* by Bernard Ferguson, and *Arnhem Lift* by a Glider Pilot. I could mention a number of others—all of them first-class reading and magnificent studies of men—books like Guy Gibson's *Enemy Coast Ahead*, Kennedy Shaw's *Long-range Desert Group*, and Malcolm James's *Born of the Desert*. If you're tempted to lose faith in man at his best read these books and remember in these days of increasing selfishness and bad manners the saying of William Morris quoted by Dr. James: 'Forsooth, brothers, fellowship is heaven and lack of fellowship is hell; fellowship is life, and lack of fellowship is death; and the deeds that ye do upon the earth, it is for the fellowship's sake that ye do them.' Fellowship—that's one of our great words for these and all days—and these are the stories of good fellowship.

Among many other thoughts I had while reading the last two books I've mentioned—*Long-range Desert Group* and *Born of the Desert*—the name of a certain oasis in Libya brought back something to my mind. It is the Siwa oasis which is also known as the Oasis of Ammon or Jupiter Ammon. I remember when first I saw in Egypt a man with the word 'Senussi' on his shoulder—and what a thrill it gave me to think that these gallant warriors were on our side; and the Siwa

The Matterhorn

Oasis is largely dominated by this great fighting clan.

Now I don't know what your idea of an oasis is, but I used to think of an oasis as a rather small bit of fertile ground —about the size of a washing-green with a couple of palm-trees and, of course, some water. Be that as it may, certainly the Siwa Oasis isn't like that at all. It's about six miles long and nearly five miles wide and almost four thousand people live in it. It's very fertile, and its old name meant 'Palm Land', and it's famous for its dates—the best in Egypt; and even in Tripoli the Arabs say 'Ya Tamr Siwa'—'Oh for the dates of Siwa!' It was there that the Long Range Desert Group had their headquarters for a time.

Now, why am I talking about Siwa and why did it bring back memories as I read these books? Well, it brought back to me the story of Alexander the Great's famous visit to Siwa. This young warrior so long ago spent his years in conquest. You remember how Robert Burns put it in his song, 'Bonny Lesley':

> Or, saw ye bonny Lesley
> As she gaed o'er the Border?
> She's gane like Alexander
> To spread her conquests further.

Well, Alexander the Great had come to Egypt to 'spread his conquests further'. He came with his architect and ordered him to build between the sea and the lake a great town in the Greek style, and called it Alexandria after himself. He was a Greek at heart and wanted to spread Greek culture and civilization wherever he went. So after conquering Asia Minor, Syria, Palestine, and wrestling Egypt from the Persians, he saw the great city started, and then with some of his companions set out across the Western Desert, now so well known to thousands of men. Out into the wilds of the Desert he went, leaving civilization behind him, and rode in those summer days to the Oasis of Siwa.

D

The somewhat biased historians of these days tell us how, in crossing the baking hot desert with blue sky and desert rats and gazelles running from him, flocks of birds sheltered him with their wings and guided him to Siwa.

When he got there he went to visit a lonely and mysteriously lovely shrine. He, the greatest man of his age, had succeeded in reaching this wild out-of-the-way place; he, the Great Alexander, had come. He was just twenty-five years old—and then took place the now famous scene, for the story goes that the priest of the Temple came out and saluted the young tourist. He called him the 'Son of God'. Alexander, pleased at this, then asked if he would become the King of all the world. The Priest said he would. His friends were a bit shattered at this and quite naturally asked if they should worship him and they were told that they should. What really took place is not quite clear. Some say that the Priest's Greek was inaccurate—what he meant to say was 'paidion', which means 'my child', and what he naturally said was 'Paidios', the Greek for 'O Son of God'. —a very natural confusion—but with quite different meanings! Whatever happened, from the time he left Siwa Alexander was never the same: as the monk prefaced his story on Chaucer's Canterbury Tales, 'that every wight that hath discretion hath heard somewhat or all of his fortune'.

Well, most of us have heard somewhat of his fortune. Greece no longer became the centre of the world he set out to conquer. He 'flung himself again but in a new spirit as against the might of Persia—he fought her as a lover now'. So Persia was crushed and India's turn was next. After that it would be Rome, and he could have sailed westward until he had conquered the night, and then he'd go east and conquer the day. No one can deny his courage, his energy, his splendid imagination. He was a great master of war, a great leader of men, but he never saw life steadily. He had caught a glimpse that day at the Siwa Oasis of something great and dangerous. He died at the age of thirty-three, when 'the expedition that he did most seek' and in which he couldn't conquer, stole toward him in the summer-house at Babylon.

A young conqueror he was of thirty-three whose kingdom —so great—was soon to vanish into the pages of history.

Now I wonder if by any chance any of you are thinking just now what I'm thinking. Thinking, that is, of another young conqueror of thirty-three whose kingdom, so different, increases with the years. Yes, Jesus of Nazareth too died at the age of thirty-three, and a great conqueror He was—not of territory, but of the hearts of man, and of His Kingdom there is no end for He conquers still. He too was called the Son of God—and there was no mistake about it this time; nor did He need to set out to conquer the night or the day—for He claimed from the first to be Lord of both. He too had courage and energy and vision. Yes, and surely even in these materialistic days we can say of Him too what Chaucer's monk said of Alexander—remember again: 'that every wight that hath discretion hath heard somewhat or all of his fortune'.

To compare these two conquerors is to compare leadership at the very highest level and at the same time to see how quite hopeless is the comparison—one the mighty warrior prince with the whole world at his mercy—the other, the peasant Prince of Peace whose Kingdom was not of this world. Yet it is the mighty warrior prince whose kingdom is an episode in ancient history, and the peasant Prince of Peace whose Kingdom is without end. A strange thing perhaps, but who can deny its truth?

Perhaps the secret lies in finding from where each got his authority. Each was a great leader for the purpose to which he was leading men; but the purpose differed and that was due to the authority behind each. It's an extraordinary thing really, is authority. Has it ever struck you how it is that a policeman has only to hold up his hand to stop the most powerful of cars and processions, and yet when he goes home he may find that his small son of twelve is not nearly so easy to manage. A judge can sentence the toughest of criminals to prison and brook no contempt of court, and yet be completely overruled by his daughter who tells him he's 'old-fashioned and not to be silly'; and as for Colonel Blimp at whose words a thousand men move as one—wait till he gets home and takes his orders from that frail old wife of his! When the policeman stops the procession or the judge passes sentence or the colonel orders his troops, each does it and gets instant action because of the authority behind him—the authority of the law or the crown or whatever it is. Each becomes an instrument of something great outside himself: and therein lies the secret that makes the authority of Alexander the Great and his kind so temporary and so different from those who have the authority of Jesus of Nazareth and those who follow Him. One is the temporary authority of an earthly power, the other is the Eternal authority of God.

The Church as it should be (for only then after all is it the Church and not a sham imitation of it) speaks with the authoritative voice of God, without compromise, fear, or favour. It certainly is Eternal and unchallengeable. The Body of Christ can only speak with the eternal authority of God. John Knox said from the pulpit of Stirling: 'It is the eternal truth of the Eternal God that we maintain. It may be oppressed for a time but in the end it will ultimately triumph', and: 'The eternal truth of the Eternal God' is the Word of God—and that is the Church's authority.

In the last area in which our Division was stationed before I left Italy we had a Brigade at Pavia, which I sometimes used to visit. It's a fine old town with a famous university; but for me this place will always be associated with an answer once given by a soldier. After the Battle of Pavia, a

Frenchman who had been captured was brought before the Emperor, Charles the Fifth of Spain. The Emperor asked the soldier how many days' march were his frontiers distant from Paris. The young French soldier drew himself up and saluted the Emperor and said: 'Twelve days, your Majesty, twelve days, but they will be twelve days of battle, Sir.'

I don't know how many days' march you and I still have till we reach the goal of our journey's end. I can only hope that each will be a day of battle, and though we may be oppressed for a time, in the end we will ultimately triumph. Each a day of battle, for only then will they be days of peace.

Let me then finish with an extract from a letter once sent to the men of Ephesus.

I have no more to say, brethren, except this, draw your strength from the Lord, from that mastery which his power supplies. You must wear all the weapons in God's armoury if you would find strength to resist the cunning of the Devil. It is not against flesh and blood that we enter into the lists, we have to do with princedoms and powers with those who have the mastery of the world in these dark days with malign influences in an order higher than ours. Take up all God's armour then so you will be able to stand your ground when the evil days come and be found still on your feet when the task is over. . . . With all this take up the shield of faith, with which you will be able to quench all the fire-tipped arrows of your wicked enemy, and take the sword of the spirit which is the Word of God.

Yes, every day a battle, and life a fellowship, for remember that: 'Forsooth, brothers, fellowship is heaven and lack of fellowship is hell; fellowship is life and lack of fellowship is death; and the deeds that ye do upon the earth, it is for fellowship's sake that ye do them!'

Seven

GOD'S FIRST QUESTIONS

I think it's true to say that ever since man came on the earth he has wanted to know, to find out, he has been full of questions; but it's only within recent years that people have had an opportunity of having their questions taken seriously, especially younger people. I mean the children in the days of our fathers were not encouraged to ask questions. In fact they were quite forcibly sat on if they tried. They were told that they were either too young, or that it wasn't their business, or that they ought to take the word of older people, and so on. Now, of course, in many cases that is the best answer. But I think it is a very good sign of the times that people nowadays are not only asking more questions, but are being encouraged to ask more questions. Personally, I welcome questions about religion because I think it clears up some misunderstanding, and I think the Church has never anything to fear but has everything to gain by tackling these questions; provided, of course, that these questions are honest and sincere.

There are of course some people, usually the cynical, self-satisfied, quasi-educated type who, like the chief priests and the Scribes in the New Testament, ask, as they did, by what authority God does certain things, and these things are legion—the problem of evil and suffering, the modern interpretation of the commandments, and so on—as a form of mental gymnastics, which don't always ring true.

There's a story in the New Testament about some of these

44

men who came to our Lord and asked Him by what authority He did certain things, and after they had asked Him that, He didn't give them an answer, but said: 'Now I'm going to ask *you* a question, and if you answer that question, then I'll tell you by what authority I do these things.' You can read all about that in the eleventh chapter of St. Mark.

Of course not all people are cynical—in fact the vast majority aren't—and most people are sincere, and most of the questions we are asked are asked sincerely, and hopefully, and I hope we try to answer them sincerely too. We certainly *are* asked questions as many of you know. I don't think ever before in the history of our country have so many questions been asked about religion. To help that we have to thank that wonderful opportunity that is given to most of our units in the Army today, the child of the Guards and of the Airborne Division, which is called the Padre's Hour. But in the Army I found that the questions were not limited only to the Padre's Hour. Curiously enough, I found I was asked more questions about religion at Troops' dances than almost anywhere else!

Now it's quite right, as I've said, for people to ask questions, but as Our Lord showed us, it's sometimes a very good thing for us to answer some questions before we ask any more, or rather before we expect an answer to some of the ones we ask ; and perhaps the way to find out by what authority God does certain things is to listen to Him again saying to us: 'Now you answer Me this, and I will tell you by what authority I do these things.' So let's look back a bit and see what the first three questions are that the Bible tells us that God asked man.

Right then, here's the first. 'Man, where are you?' Actually, the word is Adam, but as you all know, or ought to know, because it's been told people often enough, Adam is the Hebrew word for man, and the Old Testament, as we know it, is a translation from the Hebrew. Well then, there's the first question—and can you and I answer it? Where are you? Oh no, I don't mean sitting in a chair, or lying on your bed. I mean where are you in your relationship to God? When man was asked that question he was hiding from God. He was just being an ass—and not even an ass can hide anything from God. Actually in the story he was hiding in a bush, and he thought he was safe. No! you can't hide from God. And we're all of us, all the time, trying to hide from Him, because we're all of us really, when it comes to the bit, asses at times. There's nothing we can hide from God ever. So God faces us again now; yes now, just where we are, faces us again with the challenging question—'Where are you in your relationship with Me? I know what you're hiding, but you know I see it all the time. Come on now, stand on your feet. Come out into the open, and be a man.' Well, answer that question, will you, each one of us for himself—Where are you?

Now for the second question, and this time it's a question I find God asking Cain—'Where is your brother?' That's another challenging question to you and to me now. 'Where is your brother?' Cain, who was the first murderer, tried to answer it, you remember, by saying: 'Am I my brother's keeper?' And that's how most of us answer it to this day. 'Where is your brother?' One of the good things that comes out of a war is that we do begin to understand better our fellow men. I heard a Member of Parliament say (a Member of Parliament who came from a Christian home, who had been President of the Oxford Union, joined the Army as a sapper, and later received his commission), at a large public meeting, that he'd found far more practical Christianity in a Nissen hut than anywhere else in his life before. I think most of us would agree with him there. On the whole, people did think more about each other in the Services than ever they did before. The same cause and roughly the same uniform, among many other things that are the same, do help us to see people as they are, and not as we imagined them to be before. I met a young soldier who came from Borstal, doing a guard with a young soldier who came from one of England's most famous public schools, and they were the very best of friends; and it was real friendship, none of your superficial stuff. Again, in civvy life, just look how things have changed. It required only a band of cloth with L.D.V. on it to bring together, in 1940, Mr. Smith and Mr. Jones, who before 1939 had never spoken to each other. It was a siren that made Mrs. Snooks, who owns the big house, and Mrs. Brown, who scrubs the stairs, meet; it was a siren that brought them together, and made them better able to understand each other, and made them see how nice the other really was. For it was Mrs. Snooks who afterwards made tea for Mrs. Brown. Oh yes, war's a great mixer, and people do begin to see each other with a more friendly eye. I must say it gave me tremendous pleasure sometimes to see the fellow who used to go to the office every morning in a Rolls, pedalling along on a second-hand bicycle—and I think on the whole *he* enjoyed it tremendously too. But is this going to last? Sometimes, now that the war is over, one begins to wonder. When Cain gave the modern man's answer: 'Am I my brother's keeper?' God ignored the answer, and said: 'What have you done with your brother?'

> *Thou who art Lord of all the tender pities,*
> *Mercy Incarnate, human and divine,*
> *How could we write Thy name upon these cities*
> *Wherein Thy children live like herded swine?*

> *Would not those eyes that saw their angels gazing*
> *Into the brightness of the Father's face,*
> *Turn on this slum with love and fury blazing,*
> *Shrivelling our souls with shame of such a place?*

Where are My children, those the Father gave you?
What have you done with babes that bore My name?
Was it for this I suffered so to save you?
Must I for ever burn for you in shame?[1]

Where is your brother? Do you really care? Yes, on the whole we have begun to care. But don't let us stop now. For if we do, then will we once more remember that Cain's answer is not the right one. 'Am I my brother's keeper?' No man who calls himself a Christian should ever really hate anyone, though of course he must hate, and hate often with a bitter hatred, much they do. Our Lord always taught us to try to save the sinner by condemning the sin, but all the time remember the often-hidden loveliness in every man and woman. There's a story in the Bible about casting the first stone, which we all ought to remember. 'One of the distinguishing marks of the Church of Christ', says Professor John Baillie, 'is its attitude to the outside.' So then there's the second question which we must answer each for ourselves: 'Where is your brother?'

The third question in the Bible that I'd like us to answer tonight is a question that God asked Moses once—'What have you got in your hand?' Now Moses was a very wonderful man. Quite one of the greatest men that has ever lived, but don't run away with the idea that he was always like that, because he wasn't. He'd had a none-too-pleasant past. He'd fled from justice. He'd never known the joys of a real home life. He was living with his wife's relations, and he didn't get on very well with his wife—he'd a nagging wife, though his father-in-law seemed to like him. As Martin Luther once said: 'Poor Moses was the most plagued of men.' He was a very ordinary man at this time when God spoke to him, doing a very ordinary job, with little or no advancement, and yet he was chosen by God to do a great

[1] Studdert Kennedy, 'The Unutterable Beauty'.

job, and he began to make excuses, just as we make excuses. Supposing and supposing he said I haven't got this and I haven't got that. Just the sort of things we say. We know God won't listen to these excuses. He didn't want to know what Moses hadn't got. He asked him what he had. God doesn't want to know what you and I haven't got. He asks us what, simply, we have got. 'What have you got in your hand?' Well, I grant you, some of us may not have much —but God means us to use what we have. And what lovely and precious things most of us do have really; we've life and the assurance of God; we can pray and we can laugh— thank God we can laugh. And we have friends, and those who love us, and we can be kind to all we meet. Do you remember some of the things that Rupert Brooke loved: 'These I have loved' he said:

> *White plates and cups, clean-gleaming,*
> *Ringed with blue lines; and feathery, fiery dust;*
> *Wet roofs, beneath the lamplight; the strong crust*
> *Of friendly bread; and many-tasting food;*
> *Rainbows; and the blue bitter smoke of wood;*
> *And radiant raindrops couching in cool flowers;*
> *And flowers themselves, that sway through sunny hours.*

Well we've got all these, except perhaps at the moment the 'many-tasting food' bit. Another thing the war surely has shown us is that we're able to get on today without so many things we thought we never could get on without before; and on the whole we're really remarkably fit and remarkably happy. The little and seemingly unimportant things matter so much now, and it's these little things that we so seldom ever think about which really make up our lives. In a hut not long ago I came across an old copy of the *Spectator* (June 1935), and in it there was an anonymous poem. It seems to say much better what I've been saying. Here's the poem now:

Give me the little common joys:
The Sunday rest from labour,
A simple book, a pleasant look,
'Good morning' from good neighbours.

In little common daily things,
Always my truest bliss is:
A prayer to God, a sleepy nod,
And children's sudden kisses.

And as in little things we have, so in the little things we do. It's really in the little things, you know, that we show what we're like. In the long run it's the little things that count, that make *me* me, and *you* you, for generally speaking in the bigger things, most of us are the same. 'What have you got in your hand?' Well, with the things that most of us have, we can really do an awful lot today. We can all be a bit kinder to each other, for most of us are fighting a hard battle. Moses, you remember, was called to save God's people; and that's just what we are called to do in these hard days. To save God's people. For Moses, 'God's people' meant the Children of Israel: for us, they are the Children of God everywhere—the Kingdom of God has no foreign nation. Yes, we know now what Moses never knew, that in a strange and most wonderful way, as we do God's will in helping others, so do we do service to God Himself. 'One of these the least of My breathren' He called them. What a new dignity this gives to all our work and service:

Wide-eyed, wondering whom or what he should meet,
Robinson died and came to the judgement seat.

Saw a welcoming face that smiled in his own,
'Master, Master,' he cried, 'had I only known;

'Only believed that the story was really true,
I should have worshipped, I should have followed you.

'*I should have been your servant, and done your will.*'
*Jesus said to him: '*Nay but you served Me still.*'*

I was a sensitive child at your public school
(Have you forgotten) that you shielded from ridicule.

I was the passionate boy that you didn't tease,
I was the awkward lout that you put at ease.

I was the factory lad that you taught to play
After your office hours on a Saturday.

I was the hungry people you clothed and fed
I was the lonely bores that you visited.

Mine were the trivial faults to which you were blind
I was the German clerk to whom you were kind.

Whenever you fought for justice I fought with you
Whenever you pleaded for pity I pleaded too.

Now there is other work on the harvest land
Awaiting for you to do. Give me your hand.'[1]

Very well, then, three questions for us all tonight—
Where are you in your relationship to God? Where is your
brother? And what have you got?

But, having *answered* these, then *ask* some questions.
There's no harm in asking—it's not a wrong thing to do.
Remember how Fr. Arthur Stanton, that most wonderful
and much-loved priest of St. Alban's, Holborn, once put it:
'When your heart is troubled, and your mind is not satis-
fied, and you are longing and longing to know these things,
don't forget the text, "Jesus knew that they were desirous
to ask Him"' (St. John xvi, 19).[2] We are poor children
crying for the light, but it is because we are children and we
are alive that we long to ask the question. Dead men never
ask questions. It is because you are alive, and your soul is

[1] G. F. Bradby.   [2] *Faithful Stewardship.*

alive, and your heart is alive, and tears mount to your eye, that you long to know that which is above and about you. 'Jesus knew that they were desirous . . .' He knows that you are longing to understand and to love His word. 'Hereafter—hereafter, ye shall see the Son of Man—hereafter ye shall know.' Stand back and look out in eternity, and remember, 'Hereafter'. There is a large word for you! 'Hereafter'—it stretches across the whole horizon of your thoughts and inquiries. 'Ye shall know even as ye are known.' Live quietly now to God and think of the eternal years. And remember these three questions—and let's be honest with ourselves!

Eight

AN OLD SHEPHERD AND THE YOUNG DOCTOR

I never met Dr. James Walker Dawson of Edinburgh. Yet now I seem to know him as I'd know a friend. For quite recently Mr. Robert Grant gave me a copy of two of his lectures to his students—not lectures on medicine but on life. They are called 'The Spirit of Leisure' and 'The Spirit of Work': and I'm glad that the lectures are in that order for as I've pointed out before, what we do with our leisure time is really more important to ourselves than what we do in our work. Our leisure time—which we must never confuse with our *idle* time—has more than anything else to do with the formation of our life and character. And so I'm glad that Dr. Dawson spoke on the Spirit of Leisure before he spoke on the Spirit of Work.

Leisure I've said before, and Dr. Dawson reminds us again, should be so used as to render us fit and strong for our work. Yet though leisure is so importnat, the paradox is that there *can* be no real leisure unless there is real work. And real life is a blended combination of the two.

This, of course, is where the need of the right sort of education comes in—whether it is in the home or the school or for those who leave school young in such organizations as clubs, brigades, or scouts. For education should teach people before all else to—in Plato's famous definition—'feel pleasure and pain at the right things'[1]—or in the now

[1] Goodness of character has to do with pleasure and pains. It is pleasure that makes us do what is bad and pain that makes us abstain from what is right. That is why we require to be trained from our earliest youth, as Plato has it, to feel pleasure and pain at the right things. True education is just that.—Aristotle.

53

almost hackneyed words of Arnold's description of Sophocles when he wrote that 'he saw life steadily and saw it whole'.

One of the chief troubles today is that people's thinking becomes so one-sided or inconsidered and problems are 'summed up' in words like 'capitalism' or 'communism' without balancing for a moment what these words mean.

For myself, I cannot help but feel that if we want to train men and women to use their leisure and to blend it rightly with their work, these two precepts must be ever before us —'to feel pleasure and pain at the right things' and 'to see life steadily and see it whole'.

Now in the second of these lectures of Dr. Dawson's—the lecture on the 'Spirit of Work'—he tells how once when he was spending a short holiday on the Cairngorms, in the deepening twilight of an evening, he met an old shepherd sitting on the hillside, his dog beside him. This old shepherd, he says, was looking away every now and then on to the hills opposite, with a telescope, chatting as he did so to his dog, who seemed to be as anxious as his master. Dr. Dawson sat down beside them and asked if he had lost a sheep. Yes he'd lost some sheep. The Doctor then offered to take the sheepdog—if it would go with him—and round them up for the old man. But this wasn't what the shepherd wanted, all he wanted to know was where they were. The Doctor then took the telescope and putting it to his eye, searched the hills for some time and eventually found the sheep, and gave the shepherd a description of them. And then as the Doctor handed back the telescope the old shepherd very politely turned to him and said: 'And what, sir, might be your vocation?' He said he was a Doctor; and then, said the old man, 'But you know nothing about sheep?' The Doctor explained that he did because he was once a shepherd in New Zealand. Then gently and kindly but somewhat reproachfully the old shepherd turned on him and asked: 'And what made you give up that vocation?'

Asolo, Italy

'And what made you give up that vocation.' These words recalled something to the Doctor's mind. Three words that a man writing in the Middle Ages had said summing up a man's life—three Latin words: '*vocatio, tentatio, oratio*'. We'll come to them in a minute—but it was the first, *vocatio*, that immediately 'rang a bell'—vocation.

Well, at the old shepherd's request he spent the night with him in his cottage up the glen, for he had wandered rather far from the place he was staying in at Aviemore; and that evening before a log fire they sat and talked far into the night. The shepherd's story was a simple one. Forty years before he had brought his wife in to the glen—she who had died this very summer. It had, he said, been a 'great parting'. And 'the old man had a face into which the wonder and the beauty and the pain of life had passed'.

Can some of us—rushed, noise-worn, soot-covered, town folk just think of it—fifty years in that highland glen—quiet and peaceful almost in the words of that well-known prayer of heaven:

'The busy world is hushed, the fever of life is over . . . a safe lodging, a holy rest and peace at the last.' There they had lived the simple restful life 'away from the sordid things'.

Yet from him Dr. Dawson was to learn one of the most profound of all life's lessons. For that night the old shepherd spoke to him of his vocation—not only among the sheep in the glen but among the folk there where he and his wife had spent their days helping their neighbours in simple honest ways. He told how his wife used to go to the homes of the people—cooked for one, washed or cleaned or scrubbed for another, and as the Doctor thought of it later he was able to tell his students, 'as the old shepherd spoke of his wife, I knew that the face in the vision before him was a happy face'.

Then it dawned on him how closely allied to the first

E

word 'vocation'—*vocatio*—is the second, *tentatio*—the Latin for all that tries and thwarts us—pain, disappointment, suffering, sorrow. There's much to be done—but there is temptation to be met; and the old shepherd had blended his work with meeting the temptation in the lives of others around him.

Then the old man pleaded with the young Doctor to use his life aright. He told him what a wonderful profession a doctor's really is for the vocation of a doctor was to meet the temptations—the pain, the suffering, the sorrow—in other's lives.

Well, that's the story of the young doctor and the old shepherd—a story of the hills known now so well to both Highland and Lowland Divisions in this last war.

I pass it on to you, as he did to his students, because it helped me so much and I hope it will help you too a bit.

Let's look at it again for a minute.

There's that word *vocation*. How seldom—how all too seldom do we find it in people's minds or on their lips today. How often 'what's the pay, the "screw", the stipend, the working-hours, the pension at the end', and how seldom, now, 'what's the opportunity for helping, for doing a finished job, for filling my niche in the world, *giving*'. With how little vision, consecration, do we consider the work we are called to do in this world. Keats in a now famous letter calls this world 'the vale of soul-making'. 'And', said a greater man than Keats, 'what shall it profit a man if he gain the whole world and lose his soul?' The calling of the shepherd is every bit as much a vocation as the calling of the doctor; the calling of the bricklayer or the calling of a parson. Indeed can it not be said in these days when so many are 'not coming back', can it not be said that we who are left (and sometimes we ask why *we* are left) have each a vocation here and now in our leisure hours at least—if we find it hard to seek it in our working hours?

'It is for us, the living, rather to be dedicated here to the unfinished work . . . dedicated to the great task remaining before us . . . that we here highly resolve that the dead shall not have died in vain'—said Lincoln at the dedication of the battlefield of Gettysburg—but words that might easily be spoken at the United Nations' Organization, or in any works or office or study today.

Perhaps, you say, 'my work doesn't allow for vocation— it's just not that kind of a job'—'no one could call my work vocation' and perhaps you are right. But perhaps if such is the case your vocation is to be there all the same—possibly to 'test' you all the better in the 'vale' that Keats spoke of, and certainly to make your vocation as the old shepherd and his wife did, to meet the *tentatio*—the sorrow, the pain, the disappointments, the difficulties, yes—the same word— the temptation in others' lives.

Yet the word *tentatio* really means more than that (though all these are included), it means all that *disciplines* us; and though the word discipline smacks a bit of 'old Stinker' at school or the R.S.M. it really means the rule by which we live and govern our lives. Without discipline no one really lives in the fullest sense of the word.[1] The translation of the Latin motto of Melville College in Edinburgh means 'discipline develops character': and without character man is little different from the beasts.

Where there is light there must be shadow, but only those who face the light have their shadows behind them. It is, as I've said, every man's vocation to meet this temptation which disciplines in other men's lives, but to meet it we must ourselves know the answer, must ourselves know the pleasure *and pain* at the right things. Over the entrance to one of the big London hospitals you can read these words from the Latin: 'I learn how to treat

---

[1] I am here reminded again of General Sir Neil Ritchie's definition of Discipline: 'Discipline', he said to me, 'is unselfishness.'

my patients, knowing what it is to be ill myself.'

Have you known what it is sometimes to be in sorrow, to be disappointed, to be in pain, to feel you've failed? Well, you can now all the better turn that to your good and to the good of others. 'He has not learnt the discipline of life', said Emerson once, 'who has not known failure.'

For every man, as I reminded you in the last chapter, has not only got to ask himself where he is with God, what and where he is trying in his foolishness to hide from God, he has also to answer: 'Am I my brother's keeper?'

That brings us to the third Latin word, which some of you may remember mentioned—the word *oratio*, which translated freely means communion with God. Yes. I have come back to that again, because you can't leave it out. You can't—well, my friend A. C. F. Beales told me the other day about a man who took three double whiskies and soda and got drunk, so next night he thought he'd better take something else, so he took three double brandies and soda and again got drunk. He thought the matter over and decided that as the only thing common to them both was the soda; it must have been the soda that made him drunk, so he decided to leave that alone in future. Now, if you apply that to the present-day you'll begin to see what's happening—take, for example, the two stock phrases facism and communism. Each started with a 'touch' of Christianity and each set the world quite mad. So they blamed the Christianity and took each neat—which led to war and all its attendant horrors.

Oh, not a very good example, I admit; but the point is that the one thing that is needed to see life steadily and whole is just that which has been and is still being discarded. A man's vocation if he is to see it aright, a man's discipline in temptation both for himself and in others must be bound up in his communion with God—this communion which comes to all of us once and for all through Jesus Christ.

Once—some years ago now—I put to you the three great petitions of Robert Louis Stevenson: 'Give us courage and gaiety and the quiet mind.' At that time we were holding grimly on in war and the bombs were falling hard on London. After that talk a flying bomb fell, blinding a worker with the blast of glass. As he was being carried to hospital, bruised and battered and blind, he turned to one of those who bore him in and murmured 'Courage, gaiety, and the quiet mind"—that's what the Padre said, "Courage, gaiety, and the quiet mind".' I have broadcast well over one hundred and fifty talks and I can truthfully say that it has all been worth it for that one man alone.

Dare I even hope that perhaps one man, one woman, now might say vocation—what I can put into my job, what I am called to do even perhaps in spite of what the job is like—brother Lawrence you remember found his vocation in the kitchen: discipline in temptation—self-discipline, ordering my life aright, discipline in helping others to face temptation and come out triumphantly; *oratio*—yes I'm going to begin *now* to—well, to say my prayers tonight, however shortly, but certainly sincerely, I'm going to get into touch again with my Father God. In other words, I'm going to begin to feel pleasure and pain at the right things and begin again to see life steadily and see it whole —as, yes—as God will have me see it.

So will we pass out of the vale of soul-making into the glory of His presence as men who because they can get down on their knees, can stand upon their feet—so will we have *lived* and not 'waffled' through life—so will our life have a purpose, a rule, and end. There we will find with the secret of life, the secret of happiness, and after all, that's worth finding, isn't it?

Nine

'STARTING FRESH IN THE MORNING'

I remember so well the evening he came to see me—looking so young, bronzed, and fit, with shorts and open-necked shirt, straightening up his cap which had been on the back of his head. As he came towards my caravan, he came up to me and said: 'Say, mate, can you tell me where the padre is—Selby Wright, you know.' I replied: 'I'm the padre—although I admit I hardly look like it, and what can I do for you, old man.' He looked a bit flabbergasted and said: 'Sorry, sir, sorry to bother you', and all that sort of thing. Then he told me that he'd come from an outlying unit that didn't at that time have a padre, and he wanted to talk about something that was worrying him a lot. He thought that perhaps a padre could help him, and so hearing a truck was going to Divisional Headquarters he'd got a lift. So he sat down and we talked together.

It was the same old story. A fine-living fellow who just wanted to get something off his chest, and with a real desire to make a fresh start wanting some assurance that it would be forgiven. It's the same story that every minister and priest could tell.

But when all is said and done, the thing that really matters is the personal touch—the friendly chat, the quiet reasoning, the gradual unfolding of a point not understood so far—and it's just that which is missing in letters to and from people that we have never met and don't really know. But there is one thing about so many of the letters I receive—the large number of people who write to me just *because* they don't know me personally and just because though in some real way to them we seem to have become friends on the wireless they are never likely to see me, they pour out their souls in a way that otherwise they wouldn't dream of doing. It is a sign of the real loneliness that is common if truth be told to most folk, the longing to tell others, the longing to 'get it off our chests'. Perhaps it is better to put it bluntly and briefly—there is an almost universal feeling among us all of guilt which leads to the desire to confess—or justify —what we don't like to call our sins in a way that often very understandably is not going to give more away than we can help; and this confession is made partly for its own sake as a kind of safety valve in case the engine bursts, but more strongly as a prelude to the very real desire deep down in every man for forgiveness. I think that behind by far the most of the letters there is that. So I think that perhaps it might help just a little bit both those who have been good enough to write and those who have been good enough not to write, if I talked about this whole business about confessing our sins, and getting ourselves right again.

Your sins probably differ a bit from mine, and mine differ possibly each day—that is why we should some time each day confess our sins, mentioning them each one, to God, and ask for strength to try not to do it again. For example, there is the sin of which far too many of us are guilty—the sin of jealousy—just about one of the most damnable of all sins. Most of us in a greater or less degree may be selfish, and there is no question about that too being a sin; it's a sin to waste things that men have risked or given their lives to bring to us, and it's a sin to waste time whether other people's or your own. When we've confessed these sins we've only just begun. Then there are sins which aren't really personal to us as individuals but we must all admit our share in them; the sin of poverty in plenty, slums and bad housing, war, drunkenness, the women who walk our streets. Then perhaps you and I have got some very personal things—known only to us and to God. The word is sin and there is no use beating about the bush and calling it anything else. If we fail to do the will of God or refuse to do the will of God once again we sin. You see that sin always in the long run refers back to God and always must; it isn't a 'matter of opinion'. It is something that is quite definite and the consequences are quite definite too. But I'm not going to talk about the consequences tonight—I'm going to talk about why we should confess these sins and get rid of them, and so make ourselves and our neighbours and God who created us happy.

Why then should we confess our sins at all, in the first place to each other? Well, somewhere in the Bible it tells us that we ought to confess our sins one to another; and when St. James tells us there that we should confess our sins to each other, he very definitely knew what he was talking about. In point of fact, everyone does confess one to another, in some degree; but only when such confession to a friend, or some other person you trust, is really made to God and not to escape God, is it really of any value. Personally, I don't like people confessing their intimate sins in front of a whole mob of unknown people. It may of course be helpful, and in some cases may even be right, but too often it is an unfortunate type of exhibitionism. But real confession to someone we trust has a very real value. For one thing, it lets off a safety valve, and for another you very often find that you're not as alone in the world as you thought you were. And, too, you have a wonderful new feeling of a confidence that somebody else shares with you. They can't of themselves pardon you; only God can do that; but they can help you tremendously in other ways.

There, then, are a few reasons why we should confess to

each other. But why should we confess to God? I mean, after all, why should we tell God who knows that we have done wrong—why should we tell Him what He knows already? He knows the secrets of all men's hearts, and even hears our thoughts. Why tell Him, then? Well, there's a very good reason why we should tell Him. Let's put it this way—suppose that your wife, or a friend, were to come to you and say: 'I didn't tell you I was sorry. After all, you must have *known* that I was.' What would your answer be? Or who would be so foolish as to make the excuse: 'He knew that I did it. Therefore, I didn't say anything about it'? Well, we can hardly do less with God. Again, it is a test. It is not so much telling God *that* we have sinned. He knows that already. Rather is it letting God and ourselves know that we confess that we have sinned and that we are really and truly sorry for that sin. For no sin is forgiven unless it is confessed and repented of. No one can be forgiven if they see no need for forgiveness. I once talked to you about that when I talked to you about the unforgivable sin[1]—the sin that can't be forgiven because you don't ask for forgiveness.

Now comes the point. Having confessed, is our sin then always pardoned? Are we always forgiven? The answer I give to that is 'Always', if our confession is real. But do let us remember that to be forgiven seldom means simply to be 'let off'. For example, a father may forgive his son and probably beat him as well; and most self-respecting sons would agree—not at the moment, of course, but in the long run certainly—that the father was right. Of course, I said our confession must be real confession. We must be really and truly sorry. There's no use saying we're sorry unless we mean that, God helping us—and in good things God will always help us—we will never do it again. The prayer of St. Augustine in his young days is the prayer of most of

[1] In *The Greater Victory* (Longmans, Green).

us all our days: 'Oh God, make us good, but not yet.' When I said that we should mean that we're sorry, we must remember too that the confession must be unconditional. I mean, there must be no excuses—'I wouldn't have done it if I'd known', or 'if I were sober', or any other excuse you can think of. The point is that as often as not we ought to have known—and you ought to have been sober. By all means, let us bring in the ignorance and the additional wrongs into our confession to God, but never let them become excuses.

Then, too, we must ask God to forgive us our sins only as we forgive them that sin against us. There's no earthly use expecting God to forgive us if we ourselves refuse to forgive our fellows; and *not* please like Mr. Collins in *Pride and Prejudice* who said: 'You ought certainly to forgive them as a Christian, but never admit them in your sight or allow their names to be mentioned in your hearing.' . . . I know it may certainly be very difficult to forget. We may still be aware of the sin, and be conscious and always remain conscious that it once happened. But what must always utterly change for us is that the way we look at it now, or think of it, must be quite different from the way we thought of it before he'd forgiven or *been* forgiven, and the person who is injured has completely stopped thinking of the past event as something that should come between himself and his neighbour, the self and the neighbour are now at peace. And *in this sense* all true forgiveness forgets the guilt which it pardoned. *In this sense* we must forgive if we wish to be forgiven, and we all know that an unforgiven man is of all men the most wretched. If you've done anyone any wrong, say, taken away from him anything—whether it be his spanner, his wife, or his character—we must do all we can to put this right; all we can, I said. It's not always easy, God knows; it's hardly ever easy. But unless we do all this and a great deal more which each of us knows about in his own heart, we have not fulfilled our conditions for being at one with God.

How, then, do we know when we are forgiven? I think that only those who know what forgiveness means can answer that, really. But never let any of us forget this—that the nearer we are to God the more do we see the need for His forgiveness every day. The saint is nearly always far more conscious of his sin than the sinner. You know the hymn which says:

> And those who fain would serve Thee best
> Are conscious most of wrong within.

I think that the answer is best summed up in the words of one of my former teachers, Professor H. R. Mackintosh: 'To long,' he said, 'to long for peace with the Father is to have it. . . . The forgiven man finds himself drawn close to the Father's heart.' So, you see, in our very longing to be forgiven, to give up and keep on giving up all that estranges us from God, we are forgiven.

God hates sin like hell—for hell is where God isn't. Yet He takes sinful men like us and calls us His friends if we do His commandments. To the fellow who feels himself so utterly cut off from God that he just feels there is no life for him, God says—yes, says again to *you* tonight: 'Rise, clasp My hand and come.' We've got to believe that and each man must believe it and do it for himself.

I can only assure you of that. I can't prove it to you, only you can prove it for yourself; or take it as an act of faith.

'Well, all that's very well,' you say, 'but you're a padre and believe all that sort of stuff, and I can't. How do you *know* that we can be forgiven as long as we are sincere?'

But you *can* believe it you know. It isn't that you can't so much as that you won't—don't want to.

For if you believe, the answer comes of itself; and we find

that we know because God Himself has told us—and there is no better answer than that, nor any more convincing.

One more word; you may remember what an utter funk St. Peter was when that Thursday night a girl said to him: 'You're a follower of Jesus, aren't you?' And he said of course, he wasn't, and he said it more than once, too. Then at the start of a new day the cock crowed, and he saw what a coward and what an ass he had been, and he burst into tears—and it takes real sorrow to make a tough man weep.

When Our Blessed Lord came back again, He said, you remember: 'Go and tell the disciples—and don't forget to tell Peter.'

You see, He was ready to start off fresh in the morning, and He's always ready.

Yes . . . always.

Ten

SECRETLY—THROUGH FEAR

When the 'Dandy Ninth' was stationed in Somerset in the early months of the war I went one day with 'Mac', my former Royal Scot driver (now a sergeant in India) and his friend Richardson to see Glastonbury.

Judging by the excited interest of the people of Glastonbury it didn't seem as though they had ever seen the kilt before and I well remember the embarrassment of these two young fellows as the folk stared at them in, I admit, as polite a way as is ever possible to stare!

I went to Glastonbury chiefly to see the old Abbey which is quite possibly the oldest British Christian Foundation; for tradition tells us that in the first century Joseph of Arimathea made a pilgrimage to this country and where Glastonbury now stands, on an island in the marshes, he constructed the first Christian church on the foundation of which was later to rise the great Abbey Church.

Joseph of Arimathea you may remember, was a rich man with real religious convictions, and was what I suppose today we might call an important public figure. We know one or two things about him—that he lived in what was then called Arimathea, but today is called Beit-Rima, near Lydda. (I remember going through this place with that grand ambassador of our Church, Duncan McGillivray, and the thrill I got when he told me that this was the old Arimathea.) We know too that he had stood out against the rest of the Council when the Council had consented to the death of Jesus of Nazareth, for we know too that he was a disciple of Jesus, but (here for us is the important bit) a disciple though secretly through fear.[1]

'A disciple though secretly through fear.' How well do we ministers and priests know what that means—not only in our own lives but in the lives of so many men and women we meet who come to see us. How often we find that that blasé young man who doesn't pretend to care, that indifferent young girl who is 'a bit of a problem', that old man who is 'beginning to drink too much'—oh dozens of others—how often do we find that when you have a talk with them, underneath it all is the thin veneer, a hollowness and unhappiness really, and that if truth be told (when truth is told) they are really disciples though secretly through fear: fear of being laughed at, fear of having their 'fun' spoiled, fear of having to start again; perhaps in certain places today even fear of persecution. Well, Joseph of Arimathea was like that: but he conquered his fear.

He conquered his fear. When he saw the death of our Lord and realized what it meant he ceased to be afraid and he went to Pilate (who wasn't a bad chap really, except that he was an ambitious young governor who was afraid of losing his job) and asked if he could have Jesus' body and bury it in his own private burying-place.

That really did require a very considerable amount of courage because Jewish law said that anyone who was executed should be buried straight away and not allowed to remain on the tree. Actually this was not a case of Jewish but of Roman law; and the usual thing there was to leave the body to decay: though the relatives could claim it. This meant that Joseph would have to acknowledge his discipleship in asking for the body and also in burying it— not 'anyhow', but in the best possible way—in new linen sheets he had specially bought, with spices, and within a

[1] St. John xix, 38.

new sepulchre he had set up possibly for himself in a garden near by.

Oh yes, most men are disciples though secretly through fear. Oh, I know they don't say their prayers every day—though some do (and not just funk prayers either, in fact, if truth be told they are more concerned to pray for those they love than for themselves). They don't read their Bibles every day—though some do; but in their hearts secretly through fear—for there is no other reason—they believe in God and they honour and respect and worship the Lord Jesus Christ and are really out to help others without trying to do it too obviously in case people think they've gone all sentimental and 'cissy'. Oh yes, in their hearts most men are disciples, bless them; but when it comes to the bit we are all a pretty weak lot really.

So Joseph of Arimathea was like that—but he conquered his fear—that we know. He came right into the open and did something about it, and tradition tells us that he came through dangerous ways to this rather savage island of ours; and there in Somerset on what was then an island or lake village he built a little wattle church and dedicated it to the Mother of our Lord. He, in the name of our Lord, made this expedition which we are told included in its number the Apostle Philip. Quite near, at Crewkerne, where our Signals were billeted, he set up his crook or cross on his return journey. Certain it is that when missionaries came in the year 166, sent at the request of King Lucius, they found this wattle church and a Christian community there. He conquered his fear and put his conquest into action. In the widest sense of the word—for there are many other senses of it—he became a missionary.

I know a lot of people nowadays don't like missionaries or the idea of missionaries. 'Why,' they say, as they smoke their pipes and drink their port or their tea or their beer, 'should we help other countries. Haven't we enough to do with our own?' You know that kind of conversation, don't you? Too well, sometimes. The answer is, of course, or perhaps better, our answer—for there are many others—because we ourselves have been helped, civilized, and educated, made human and humane through missionaries of the Cross, who risking all came to our land. Ninian at Whithorn, Columba in his coracle, others whose names we know and many others who have no memorial. Yes, 'risking all', because we were a pretty wild, tough lot in those days!

The point is you can't be a Christian (even a secret one) unless you are prepared to spread your faith. A true follower of our Lord must be in a wide or narrow sense a missionary—and as I heard Principal Curtis remind us again the other day, Great Britain has again become a mission-field.

Let's get this clear: 'Where would you and I be today if somebody else had not believed in missionaries?' Professor John Baillie has said:[1] 'What would Britain be like today if there had been no monk Augustine to come over from Rome to help us and no St. Columba to come over from Ireland and no St. Ninian? We are all proud of Britain, her traditions and achievements, but what would there ever have been of her had it not been for foreign missions?'

If we are agreed on that—or even if we are not agreed on that—where would you and I have been without the gracious influence of other folk—our parents for example, and those who 'took an interest in us', how much do we owe to them? Whenever I think of all the fine folk who have talked to me and helped and guided me from the time I was a baby I feel so tremendously grateful and always sadly conscious of the part I've to play to make up for them. You may not be able to go to Africa and India and you're probably not meant to, but you can perhaps go and

[1] *Asking Them Questions*—Second Series (Oxford University Press).

Photo by Ernest Raymond

The Carceri, that lovely little monastery

help that boys' club, that girls' club that is so badly needing leaders just now; and you can go and visit that rather boring person who is only boring really because she is lonely and unfriended; and there are some people with few and ragged clothes in Europe and you've really got some you can share; or you know perfectly well that your discipleship in your heart is through fear leading others not to the Lord of all good life but to the devil. How many young fellows of fourteen or fifteen have I seen going out fresh and fit from school to start as men in work and change in a year because of some damnable man (I speak theologically) or damnable woman in their works, and how many others have I seen led to a true sense of manhood or womanhood by the right sort of leaders? No man can live to himself and go through life as a Christian unless he acts toward others, and his actions toward others depend entirely on his belief. Studdert-Kennedy put it once as only he could put it: 'A man must always act upon his neighbour according to his master passion—his real belief.' He must always love his neighbour as he loves his God. You see it in action everywhere. A man who worships drink gives his neighbour beer: a man who worships lust gives his neighbour food for lust to feed on: the man who worships money gives his neighbour not money but the love of it.

You must spread your master passion and your master passion is your God. If you have no passion of any sort then you have no life to live and none to give away. You are not a man but just a bit of driftwood on the sea of life, tossed this way and that without a guide because you are in truth without a God.

Into this maelstrom of conflicting passions Christ comes not bringing a new law but a new passion—a new God. That's the Christian religion—the master passion for Jesus Christ.

What can save the ordinary man from damning his soul

F

and destroying his world? Here are the words of Studdert-Kennedy again: 'The piping of Professors? the books of the philosophers? the knowledge of the scientists? vague good-will and good nature? you cold-blooded saints of the study have you ever walked in the streets, have you ever lived? only a passion can conquer a passion. We must have God.' If we have God we must pass on God, and that is to be a missionary, and Britain—remember Principal Curtis again —has now again become a mission-field.

Joseph of Arimathea, a disciple though secretly through fear who conquered his fear.

As I looked at the ruins of the great Abbey at Glastonbury I saw parts that had been added in each generation. Each generation content to do its bit without seeing the whole finish. Life is like that—we are all builders or destroyers in this world—and each of us is building for those who come after us or destroying that which past generations have built. Those that built the Abbey Church knew that not in their day would they see the whole work finished—but that all they could do would be to do their bit well.

We will never in our day see the world as we want it to be but we can begin here and now to make a corner of it as glorious as we can make it—even if it is only a good foundation for others to build on when we have gone, and we will at least have done our part well, however small.

Do you remember how Olive Schreiner put it in *The Story of an African Farm*—well, it's something like this—'When we lie down tired-out other men will stand, young and fit; by the steps we have made they will climb, on the stairs we have built they will mount, they'll never know the name of the men who made them. At our clumsy work they may laugh, and if the stones roll, they will curse us.

But they will mount on *our* work; they will climb on *our* stairs!

And no man liveth unto himself or dieth unto himself.

Eleven

A DESERT CONVOY

Quite a number of years ago now, had you been there you might have seen a strange convoy moving across the desert; strange chiefly because of the kit the men were wearing and the nature of the goods they carried. They were riding on camels—for there was no mechanical transport, and, having no compass, they were finding their way by the stars, keeping their eyes particularly fixed on one set star ahead of them. This seemed to give them in no uncertain way the direction they wanted, for they were riding 'flat out' and were obviously going somewhere, and not just out for a ride or journeying aimlessly about. Judging by the clothes they were wearing, they might be going to some sort of investiture. One might even be excused for thinking that they were going to see a king, or even—though this seemed rather odd for men without an escort—that they were kings themselves.

As it happens, you would have been right both ways; for they *were* kings and they *were* going to see a King.

Yes, just about this time some years ago this strange convoy crossed the desert.

They had set out six days before, and their journey, they reckoned, was about half through. So you can see that, like today, it was just between Christmas and Twelfth Night. The Christmas decorations would still have been up—had there been any; but as yet there were none, for when this

73

convoy crossed the desert, it was the time of the very first Christmas.

For—and by now you have guessed it—those men now crossing the desert are those whom the world has come to know quite simply as the 'wise' men, and the King whom they were seeking—well, we'll come to that later.

For this was the very first Christmas; the time when our Calendar was changed—to read now 'from the first Christmas'; the time when the only true message of peace came to the simple and the wise—a new start for the world. So we remember again this old year's Sunday (a tired and weary year) as a new year is about to begin, a year—dare we say it, at last?—a year of peace.

What would we have been without that first Christmas? Hasn't it all been so lovely to have remembered it all again? The shepherds in the fields and the angels in the heavens, the Babe in the manger with the oxen standing by, the beautiful young Mother 'ever blessed among women'.

It's all so lovely, isn't it? But in its very loveliness lies its danger; in its very sentiment lies the danger of sentimentality; in its glorious light lies the danger of our being dazzled; yes, even in the most cynical's acceptance of the story, there lies the danger of not seeing the eternal truth behind the story. In our love for and admiration of the self-portrait we too often fail to see the meaning in the master mind of the artist—his very signature too often forgotten.

So Christmastime with its little extra kindnesses, its friendly happiness, its all too short return to the childlike heart, its glad remembrance of almost forgotten friends, so Christmas season becomes just a happy episode in the year —soon, all too soon, to be forgotten, and forgetting again to give in our selfish anxiety to get.

So, before we put away our decorations and Christmas cards, before the Scrooges go back to their old ways, let us look again at what some wise men did, and see if we, before it is too late, can learn some wisdom from them. Let us look again at the truth contained in the story, the truth behind the story of that strange convoy that was at this time passing through the desert those not so very long years ago.

What can we in our blindness and our foolishness learn from wise men?

This first, surely, that they saw a sight that should have been obvious for everyone to see. It was there for all to see, but others were either so blind or so preoccupied that they just didn't notice it. King Herod, for example. 'Just tell me,' said King Herod, 'when actually did this star you're talking about, when did it appear?' Oh yes, there are still folk like that—dozens and dozens of them. In fact, let's be quite honest, we're all a bit like that ourselves; either too taken up with ourselves, or too indifferent, or else waiting for something 'big' to happen.

Yet, many are the lights that point to Bethlehem; and the open desert has no fixed roads.

Do you remember—some of you—if you are listening now in Egypt or India, in Italy, Austria or Germany, in Africa, or at home—do you remember when we walked together one Christmastime before the war along the road that leads to Cockburnspath to attend the Christmas evening service? Four miles we walked along that much-loved road from my hut by the sea. It was—d'you remember?—a lovely frosty night. It was cold a bit at first, in our shorts and sweaters, and so we walked fast and talked on the way of many things—of camps and club days and future hopes and ambitions—so strangely changed by war (and five of you now will not come back again). And when there was a pause in the conversation, one would start the others off singing. The stars were very bright that night and one brighter than all the others—and someone mentioned this—

then there was a pause and a fellow began to sing: 'O Come all ye faithful'. We had seen His star and were 'come to worship Him'.

Men and women, boys and girls, can tramp the same road, can even live in the very same house, the same billet, but only some see the light that leads to Bethlehem: it may be a sad and worried face lit by a brave smile, beautiful flowers amid hideous destruction, some lovely trait in the life of a chap who has 'gone off the rails'.

> *I see His blood in every rose,*
> *And in the stars the glory of His eyes;*
> *His body gleams amid eternal snows,*
> *His tears fall from the skies.*

A bit far-fetched for some of us, perhaps—for that's a poetess writing. Though perhaps Miss Anna Bunston comes nearer:

> *Some folk, so I've heard say*
> *Put up a cross*
> *Right in the garden way*
> *To mind them of their Lord;*
> *But I, when I do see*
> *Thick apple tree*
> *An' stooping limb*
> *All spread wi' moss*
> *I think of Him*
> *And how He talks wi' me.*

'Just tell me,' said King Herod, 'when actually *did* this star appear?'

But these wise men did something else—they not only saw; *they did something about it*. They set out. True religion can never stop at looking up and admiring and even thanking God. It must ever involve putting faith into action.

There is no such thing as stagnant Christianity—there must be action.

Often and often I meet people who tell me, partly to excuse their present way of living, partly to show they are not as bad as they behave sometimes, how when they were younger they always used to go to Sunday school or sing in the choir, or say their prayers, and so on; they had seen the sign, but they never set off on the quest. So often we meet people who say that they have nothing against religion, but who are content to leave it at that. There are those who live outside the Christian Church, and yet receive from the Church all the benefits they can get, who offer up 'funk' prayers to God when things go wrong, who come to the Church when they want help from it, who expect the Church to give them Christian burial, baptize their children, and marry them: who from time to time see the light, but have never set off. Don't be one of these. Don't be a 'funk' Christian, or a stagnant Christian, or a parasite of the Church.

Right, then, they set off, and now we read they *came*. Of course, in every journey you must come somewhere. But where did these men come to? Did the light take them straight to Bethlehem? Not on your life; it led them to just the opposite kind of place altogether—to the sensual worldly palace of an Eastern Court. And that has ever been the way to Bethlehem—through trial and very real temptation, through the temptation to slackness and ease, luxury and greed, selfishness, love of power, and foul sensuality. The road to Bethlehem must ever lead to Herod's Palace. It's a test, and an important test, of the genuineness and fervour of the seekers; and many who start keen and fit and in the best of faith, and with sure hope of reaching their goal, fail just there. A young boy setting out fresh from school, a fellow starting a new job, perhaps at an Infantry Training Centre and Officer Cadets' Training Unit, among a new set of friends, or back with the old ones, all of us indeed if we are not too careful, will find ourselves trapped in Herod's Palace, or be led back there before the journey is done. I wonder if any of us are there now? Just let us think that over.

Once again at this season, *NOW*, there shines the truth of the wise men. They bid us set off across our desert of the world on the road that the light has marked out for us, they bid us leave behind the unreality, the wrong sort of worldliness, the selfishness and cruelty and jealousy, even the hatred sometimes of our fellows, the lust and greed that surrounds our minds.

When they saw the star, you remember, they 'rejoiced with exceeding great joy'. It's a really happy journey this, the only really happy journey.

One word more; you remember that when they reached the goal of their journey, these wise men offered the very best gifts they had. God wants no better gifts than ourselves, fit in every way. I don't know how many wise men there were. Tradition says there were three, and a fourth who got lost and went on searching until at the last he found the Baby not in His cradle but on His Cross. I don't know how many wise men there were; but I do know that today there are—and can be—as many as seek that road which alone brings happiness, alone has one true goal.

You remember how John Bunyan begins *The Pilgrim's Progress* by telling about a man who wanted to set out on a journey such as you and I are starting on, and how, in his perplexity another man came over to him to ask him what was wrong, whom he asked how he could set off on this journey, and the way to go. So he said, pointing his finger over a very wide field, 'Do you see yonder wicket gate?' The man said 'No.' Then said the other: 'Do you see yonder shining light?' He said: 'I think I do.' Then said the other: 'Keep that light in your eye, and

go up directly thereto, so shalt thou see the gate. . . .'
Everyone here has seen that light, however faint. Well,
let us keep that light in our eyes, and set off. 'Lord, we
have seen Thy star, and are come.' The star will go before
us until, as men of the only Real and Living Way, we reach
the end of our journey and see God face to face.

Twelve

THE ANSWER TO THE 'IF'

The New Testament is full of stories about ordinary folk who were just like us, only with different names. So from time to time I have talked to you about some of these ordinary folk to show you how like us they really are, and to let you see, perhaps, why they are mentioned at all; to let you see in other words, why the Bible still speaks to us as nothing else can, right up to the present moment as no other book can. I have deliberately chosen a rather lesser-known story in this chapter, about a rather lesser-known man.

Actually the only thing we really do know about him is that he lived in Damascus—you know, the place that Allenby captured in the last war, largely through the help of T. E. Lawrence of Arabia. But apart from the fact that he lived there, we really know nothing else about him, except that he was a Christian, or what today we might call a churchman. In our New Testaments he is called a disciple, which in those days meant the same thing, but unfortunately today doesn't mean that necessarily. Apart then from the fact that he was a Christian and lived at Damascus, we know nothing else about him, except the short story found in the Book of the Acts of the Apostles. We never heard of him before, and we never hear of him again, except where later on the story is retold. But God called this ordinary unknown man to do something. His name by the way, was Ananias but don't let that worry you. If he lived in this country he would probably be called Robertson or MacDonald or something like that. Yes, this fellow Robertson or Mac-Donald—we'll just call him that now—was called by God to do something—an ordinary chap who just went about his ordinary way.

God has called a lot of ordinary unknown men, you know, to do things. Some have responded and some have refused, and accordingly as they responded or refused so has God's Kingdom been helped or hindered. Their names don't matter a bit. It's only the response that matters.

I mean, what man of us can say who built the boat that brought St. Columba to Scotland? If he had built it badly, perhaps St. Columba might have been drowned, and the story of Scotland would have been different. Who taught Helen Keller, and who tutored John Wesley? Who screwed the nuts and bolts into the aeroplane that flew Mr. Churchill so safely on his many journeys? A bad piece of work there might have cost us his life then. Well, there are so many questions like that. You could ask about so many things. We don't know who all these people were most of us, and to most of us it doesn't really matter much.

What does matter for us and for the world is this: Suppose they had refused in some cases, or done it badly in others? That's where the difficulty comes in. That's the real crux of the matter. When God called Ananias he was quite ready to answer. 'Here I am,' he said, 'what do you want me to do?' That was good, wasn't it? Just like that —'Here I am; what do you want me to do?' But you know, most people really are only too anxious to answer God's call, but they won't all admit it. Most of us, when God tells us to do a job say, if we are really honest with ourselves: 'Here I am, ready to do what you want me to do.' It was the man he went to see later, who himself later said—'The spirit is willing *but* . . .' God knows the spirit is willing in most of us, *but*—God knows the 'but' too.

It's when we see *what* God wants us to do—well, we say after all, that's different, and we begin to make excuses, either to ourselves, or to other people. Now don't get worried about these excuses. Much better people than you or I have made excuses, but they got over it; and you and I can too. To go right back, in the old traditional story of Adam, he made his wife an excuse. It was all the woman's fault, he said. Well, that excuse is still being used. I'm not saying that there isn't often something in it; but if you think of it, it's a pretty miserable excuse, for a man with even an ounce of courage in him, to go and blame a woman.

Then Moses made excuses, you remember. Moses was a great leader, as Field-Marshal Montgomery reminded us in his lecture at St. Andrews; one of the greatest leaders the world has ever seen. But at first, before he became a leader, he began to tell God why he could not do it. Awfully stupid excuses they were, too. He said that nobody would believe him. He said he could not speak. He was inarticulate. All the same old excuses made today—they were all made by Moses. 'I can't talk about religion,' people say; 'I'm inarticulate.' But listen to them talking about the match last Saturday, or about the latest film. 'I'm a bit shy—just made that way, can't alter it.' But watch them dance the 'Big Apple' or its modern equivalent, whose name I've forgotten.

And this fellow Ananias, he made excuses why he should not do it. Moses why he *could not*, and Ananias why he *should not*. Moses forgot, of course, that as Joan of Arc put it: 'If God has told you what you *ought* to do, He has told you what you *can* do.' Ananias forgot that if God has told you what you *should* do, He has told you what you *must* do. God never gives us a weight too heavy for our shoulders, and we are always complaining why we cannot or why we should not.

Well, what did God tell this fellow to do? He told him

to go up to a certain house in a certain street where he would find a certain man. That was all. Who do you think this man was? Was it Peter or John? No, it was a man with a pretty sticky reputation. His name was Saul. Yes, old Smith, I know you are surprised. I know what you think about him. And mind you, you've pretty good grounds for thinking it. But 'Behold, he prayeth', that's how it's put in the Acts. I can't think of any better description of a man who has turned to Jesus Christ. It's really very encouraging for all of us—especially those who just aren't quite *sure* about our faith—to remember that the greatest of the Apostles, the greatest missionary the world has ever known, began, from being a militant unbeliever, in a simple child-like way. Not yet, notice, not yet, 'Behold he believeth the doctrine of the Trinity'. Not yet, 'Behold he believeth in the Virgin birth, or in Election or Redemption'. 'He prayeth.' That's how St. Paul began his new life in Christ, and we can all begin, therefore all men seek for Him really.

> I have a life in Christ to live,
> But ere I live it, must I wait
> Till learning can clear answer give
> Of this or that book's date?
>
> I have a life in Christ to live;
> I have a death in Christ to die,
> And must I wait till science give
> All doubts a full reply?
> Nay, rather, while the sea of doubt
> Is raging wildly round about,
> Questioning of life and death and sin,
> Let me but creep within
> Thy fold, O Christ, and at thy feet,
> Take but the lowest seat,
> And hear the Father's voice repeat,
> In gentlest accents, heavenly sweet,

Come unto me and rest;
Believe me and be blest.

Just two simple words: 'He prayeth.' But, you know,
these two words bridge a gap in a man's life between Hell
and Heaven. And our friend Ananias, like any ordinary
man, began to explain why he shouldn't go. 'I've heard,'
he says, 'I've heard about this man, how much evil he has
done.' There's something strangely familiar about these
words, isn't there? In different words, or even in the same
words, they are used so often today. They are used in
thousands of places—in men's coffee rooms, at women's tea
parties, in canteens, and at the doors of our churches after
the worship of God on Sundays. 'Have you heard about
this man—this woman?' 'I've heard and what's more . . .'
Even suppose what you say *is* true, and how seldom it is
the real truth, but even supposing it is true—and it certainly
was the case as far as the man in this case was concerned—
there is no man and there is no woman living who is ever
past praying for, and perhaps it is God's call to you, you
Mr. Smith, you Mrs. Jones, Captain or Colonel, or whatever your rank is, or whatever your name is. Perhaps it's
God's call for you to be his instrument in this. Perhaps it's
God calling you now and you say: 'Oh, that man—that
woman. I've heard . . .' Well, just remember that God
hates folk who speak like that, and God just won't listen.
'Go thy way,' He said to Ananias; 'do what you're told,
man.' That's God's answer.

Now, supposing, supposing he'd refused. You know he
could have refused. Any man, any woman can refuse to do
God's will. If— If— Well, I read the other day two
interesting things, and those two are typical of hundreds of
others. In the year 1879 there was a certain Mr. Kruger
who was working in a Government office in Africa. One
day he asked for an increase in his salary, and somebody, I

don't know who it was, somebody refused it, and he left that office. If President Kruger had got his increase in salary, well, there might never have been a Mafeking, and there might never have been a Boy Scout Movement. And in the archives of the Admiralty, I am told, there has been discovered the original application by Napoleon Bonaparte for permission to enter the British Navy. If he had become a British naval officer there would never have been a Waterloo, or a Moscow, or a Beethoven's 'Third Symphony'. Perhaps Nelson would not have stood in Trafalgar Square, for there would have been no Trafalgar. And what would have been the history of Europe? And if Ananias had refused, that might have changed and hindered God's message to the world—to you and to me, for, you see, the man he was going to see became the greatest missionary the world has ever known, the greatest missionary to the outside world. And it was all left by God, under God, to an ordinary man.

You see how He relies on ordinary fellows to do His will. Yes, you know, you and I may be delaying God's plan; I repeat delaying, for we can never in the long run thwart it. But remember this, Ananias was a disciple. His heart was all right. He knew in whom he believed. He was a bit weak, of course, but he mastered his weakness and went his way just as he had been told to do and his way was God's way. That, in the long run, is why he went it, and I bet he sang as he went along the way because at last he knew that in doing God's will he knew the great, the only real secret of true happiness. I like that bit in the story, when he got to the street, and when he got to the house, he knocked at the door, and he went in, and his opening words were, 'Brother Saul'. For they have the same Father now.

And, incidentally, what would have been the position of the world today if Hitler had answered the 'if' at Berchtesgaten in a different way?

Thirteen

The Richness of a Little Poor Man

I often sit back and thank God for my friends—the most precious possessions I have. And I like to think of heaven as a place where one is able to strengthen old friendships and make new friends: what a glorious heaven that would be, wouldn't it?

I owe so much to my friends, not only the living, and I like to think there are many, not only to those whom I knew whom we call dead—and they have become suddenly more in number than but seven years ago I'd ever thought—but also to many I've never known and never seen. Virgil and Dante are among those who we read were able to visit their departed heroes and friends—but on the whole I think they were a dull crowd, and I doubt if I should seek to look them up. Those whom I should like to see and shake by the hand and talk to and thank for all they've been to me are men like the great Montrose, Wilson of the Antarctic, and Sir Ernest Shackleton, Fr. Arthur Stanton, and most of all, Francis of Assisi.

I remember how when I first read about him in H. F. B. Mackay's little book, *The Message of St. Francis*, a new day seemed to break for me—I had a new vision of Christianity, and dare I say a new vision of Christ. Into that small frame of love and happiness of service to God and man, into that young fighter and builder, I began to see all that a man could be; perhaps most of all, though I did not quite see it at the time, I saw here a man who in G. K. Chesterton's

86

Jerusalem

words, 'Walked the world like the Pardon of God'.

And so like St. Columba I desired to 'go on a pilgrimage' one day—but my pilgrimage was to be Assisi.

The first time I saw Assisi was on a never-to-be-forgotten morning in spring. I had crossed the Appenines from Bari to Naples, travelled the famous Appian Way to Rome and then on to Perugia. From my window I could see across the plains, but when I arrived it was late evening and it was black-out. In the morning I set out with John Marshall of Renfrew and shortly after starting I saw it through the early morning mist of the Umbrian Plain, a 'city set on a hill', truly

> *. . . a city such as vision*
> *Builds . . .*

I stayed there for a week before joining my Division in the line north of Florence, but I returned to it several times later, and I feel that were I to stay there always, I'd never weary of the place. And now, in a mind stored with memories, some of the happiest I've got are of going with Robin Wood and Alan MacArthur to St. Damians or the Carceri—that lovely little monastery where still the tree stands where Francis, they say, preached to the birds; or when first I went, alone this time, to his tomb in the lower chapel of the great three-storied church which is his sepulchre. And when I returned again in the summer for another ten days the lovely blossoms had gone, but still there was a beauty there—the haze of the summer days, the ripening fruits; no black-out now for victory had come. Yet, the place was unscarred by the havoc of war, for both friend and foe had honoured and kept safe from harm this place so dear to all who love this troubadour of God who now can truly be called 'Everyman's Saint'. True from Assisi there came some unaccustomed sounds, as Bill Neill, of Aberdeen, played his pipes each night or the Scottish psalms were heard at morning and evening prayer. One could almost hear again the voice of Francis say, 'Brothers, was that not well sung', as Crimond and Martyrdom, the Auld Hundredth and French and perhaps at that time most significant of all, the old 124th rose from the little city and echoed through the Umbrian plains.

Now if one were to seek the secret of St. Francis, to ask why he has captured the hearts and lives of so many, I think one would find it in the human kinship with ordinary folk,[1] linked with an equally natural kinship to God. As Robert Burns is the poet of the ordinary man, so is St. Francis the saint of ordinary people.

For his story, you may remember, is just the story of an ordinary boy—with even more than the average boy's spirits—and he kept this happy spirit through life, but by directing it—or better, allowing his Maker to direct it— showed what real life could be like, where true happiness was to be found, and how it could all be achieved.

He was a rich young boy, remember; and he died without a penny to his name, yet probably as the richest man the world has ever known, for he came nearer to our Lord than any other man who has ever lived or loved—'the mirror of Christ', they call him.

His father, you remember, was a prosperous business man —an Assisi merchant, whose business sometimes took him into other lands; and it was while he was in France that his son was born, so he called him 'Frenchy', from which we get the name of Francis.

I cannot here go into the whole life of St. Francis—though

[1] "What gave him his extraordinary power was this: That from the Pope to the beggar, from the Sultan of Syria in his pavilion to the ragged robber crawling out of the wood, there was never a man who looked into these round eyes without being certain that Francis Bernardone was interested in him, in his own individual life from the cradle to the grave, that he himself was taken and valued seriously." G. K. Chesterton—a fine picture of true leadership.

nothing would please me more—for there is neither room nor time; and much, of course, you'll have heard or read before and the most I can do is to jog your memories. But I would suggest to you that you read it for yourself. There are some fine lives written—by Fr. Cuthbert, for instance, or Sabatier or a lighter and more fanciful book by G. K. Chesterton; and then there is H. F. B. Mackay's little book I spoke about, and also the little Plays of St. Francis by Laurence Housman.

In Sabatier's 'Life' he likens the century in which Francis lived to a young man of twenty, and the Church had become old-fashioned and 'unable to hold youth' and most of the usual jargon we hear today. 'Then Francis came and the world saw that the Church had perennial youth.'

But not at first. None could have suspected how the gay young blood of Assisi would turn out—the laughing sportsman, the leader of the smart set, this very much loved young man, who showed, too, that he had no mean head for business. At times he did some rather odd things—gave a pretty good coat once to a beggar on the road. Yet perhaps not so odd—for most fellows do things like that really when it comes to the bit. It's true he did behave rather oddly when he was a prisoner of war. He was so decent to everyone, especially to those who for one reason or another were out of the usual circle. Much as Rangers travel North to play Aberdeen, so in those days did Assisi set out to fight Perugia or other cities round about, and Francis played for the home team. A prisoner of war in Perugia, Francis was now allowed a certain amount of free time in which to think of his future. What a great future it would be! He had wealth, he had gifts, he had popularity, he had—'I shall be loved by the world'—that was his future. So, 'laughing, he rode back to Assisi and to his happy life. But he found the lights lowered, business

G*

seemed less absorbing, fun seemed less funny, gaiety less gay. He was twenty-one.'

But during his convalescence after an illness immediately following his return, the lights went up again, only to go out as on his first day out he gazed from the Porto Nuova across the slopes of the Umbrian Hills. The journey back home from that gate was his first step to the Francis we know and love. His message at this time Fr. Mackay tells us is just this: 'To die for love is a great adventure. To live for love is a far greater adventure, and this means bringing love to meet love every day in the common things of life.'

Life would always be fun for Francis, life would always be gay. The reason why the fun and the gaiety seemed to have gone was not because they were wrong, but because he had discovered that life must have purpose and direction, and only in the seeking and the finding of the right purpose and direction would the true joy of life come.

He hadn't quite got the answer yet, though, Perhaps, he thought, he ought to do something big—go on a crusade or something. Well, he was lucky, there was one just due to set off soon. Grand. So he tried on his best armour: but before the Crusade set out he had given it away to a poor fellow in a poor suit, and before the Crusade was a few days old the once gallant man of Assisi was on his way home. A dream, his conscience or maybe his imagination, told him that this was not really the way; and so he came back. The Colonel Blimps of Assisi said, of course, that it was quite monstrous, but some of the younger people who still flocked around him thought it might be love.

'That's what he needs,' said all the old ladies of Assisi, 'a wife that will settle him down a bit—I do hope he gets a nice girl and not that awful Charlotta girl'—and so on with the usual conversation that goes on in the twentieth century.

Meanwhile all the time Francis is trying to see ahead, and

to conquer those things he feared most—lepers and the haunting eyes of the poor; and all the while the gossiping went on about him.

Now Francis, like so many cheerful young fellows today. was quite a good Churchman; so he thought he'd go and see the minister and have a talk with him. His minister was the Bishop of Assisi, and he gave him the usual fatuous advice that we so often give people and told him about all the things he oughtn't to do and to pull himself together.[1]

The Bishop's advice didn't get Francis anywhere—and the poor fellow was almost in a worse state than ever; knowing what he oughtn't to do, he couldn't think what he ought to do. There are many young fellows—and those not so young—like that in the world today; and though their problems may be different, and so the answers may be different, the way to tackle them is more or less the same. And Francis tackled his first fear by being brought face to face with it. For one day when riding back from Assisi, he saw a leper standing before him—more, he was coming toward him. Here was a great crisis—he was brought face to face with what he feared most. Spurring his shying horse towards the leper, he leapt from his saddle, put his arms round the rotting body, and kissed the face now almost eaten away by disease. And next day, a stirring crowd of lepers saw a strange sight—the gay young blood of Assisi had not only come to see them but be their friend. It wasn't that Francis liked it, for though he looked cheerful as he kissed each leprous hand, the chroniclers tell how he nearly fainted with the strain and horror of it. And that's how most things we conquer feel at first, it's never really easy. 'No, I'll never do it,' you say, 'it just can't be done.'

Mr. Harry Swan, the Chairman of the Hibernian Football

---

[1] You remember what a certain old woman is reported to have said about the Ten Commandments: 'Them Ten Commandments, they don't get you anywhere—they only put ideas into your head.'

Club, showed me the other night an, it seemed, anonymous poem that someone had given him in the train:

> *Somebody said it couldn't be done,*
> *But he, with a chuckle replied:*
> *That maybe it couldn't, but he wouldn't be one*
> *Who would say so until he had tried.*
> *So he buckled right in with the trace of a grin*
> *On his face; if he worried he hid it.*
> *He started to sing as he tackled the thing*
> *That couldn't be done—and he did it.*

Good, isn't it? And that's rather what Francis did, and what you and I can do.

For having broken through and with a new vision, he went down to the little ruined chapel of St. Damian and knelt before that large and rather ugly crucifix which now you see in the Church of St. Clare. And there he gave himself to God: 'O Lord Jesus enlighten me, lift my darkness from me. Let me know you so well, that on all things I may act in your light and as you will.' A good prayer that. And the answer the gay young man of Assisi heard coming from God, 'Go build my falling-down house for me.' Well, you know what happened next; Francis took the words literally at first and began to rebuild St. Damian's, and some other churches around. Meanwhile he had quarrelled with his father, renounced his heritage, given up his old life, and become a beggar round the houses where he had formerly been a welcome guest—his only friends the lepers who loved him still. Still singing and still happy he had finished the restoration of St. Mary of the Angels, AND THEN on the day in the year 1209 at the service there he heard God speak to him in the lesson, 'Preach, saying the kingdom of God is at hand. Heal the sick, cleanse the lepers, raise the dead, cast out devils. Freely ye have received, freely give.' And dressed now in a grey-brown sacking tunic with a piece of rope for a girdle, he went up to Assisi and right up to the Market Square where the business men and dignitaries were and said: 'Brothers, the Lord give you peace.' And in silence and awe they listened to him. And from that number a great and wealthy nobleman and a distinguished lawyer threw in their lot with him; later they were joined by a young ploughboy—Giles—who was found looking for Francis in the forest and wondering if he too could be taken in. So the great movement started as a nobleman, a lawyer, a ploughboy, and St. Francis shared their bread—all gloriously happy. And the numbers grew. At first the Church didn't understand it. When nine years later the hierarchy of the Church sent a deputation to see them, they saw coming toward them not four, but five thousand brown-clad brothers. 'It is the feast of Pentecost,' said Cardinal Legate, 'and mine eyes behold the army of the Holy Ghost.' And he became lost in the army of the brothers, stripped himself of his robes and became one of them. But others were canny and more difficult. 'I do not understand your rule,' said a prince of the Church, 'you'd better take it and read it to the pigs.' Smiling Francis departed to return soon again. 'I have read it to the pigs, sir, and they don't understand it either.' Yet Pope Innocent the Third said, 'What this age needs is the spirit of the Troubadours', and later when his successor Pope Honorius said as he saw him, 'There goes a very dangerous man,' and a jealous Cardinal said, 'Indeed, I think so, Holy Father'; but, said Cardinal Ugilino—the one later to join the order—'but, dangerous to whom, Holy Father?' 'To the Devil,' said the Pope, 'Dangerous to the Devil, my son.'

So the Troubadours of God led by the Poverello sang their way through the world in the name of the Lord, and the world was to see again the perennial youth of the Church. They loved all things and all people—they spoke of 'our brother the sun, our brother the wind, our sister water, our brother fire, mother earth' even 'sister death'. Even the animals and birds returned the love they showed them—for love is just like that. And Francis died in his beloved St. Mary of the Angels, we read how 'then all the larks of the forest rose and soared. Stretching their wings and tuning their voices they gathered in a company above St. Mary of the Angels, and rose into the evening sky a circling crown of song.' Mackay in a brilliant summing-up of Francis's message to the world today includes him as saying this to us today, 'And remember you go out not to seek man, there is no such being as Man, there are only men, each called of God; each free to obey; or refuse; each unique; you go out to seek men and you go out to bring them not Christianity, there is no such thing as Christianity, it is a word coined to deceive you, you go out to bring them Christ. There is much love of Christ and desire for Christ in the world today, but nowhere is it concentrated into a terrific instrument smashing through obstacles. God has not forsaken his world, but God has given men free will, and He cannot (without denying that freedom) impose a new era upon them, they must wait to make the link with the powers who wait. Somebody must smash through.

'And the Hammer is the cross.'

Before I left Assisi on my last visit, I asked to see the famous letter that Francis wrote at the end of his life to brother Leo. At the end of the letter he had drawn a hill shaped like a skull and on it a cross which covers the horizon, a cross with no head to it no inscription on it.

It is a cross shaped like a hammer.

May I leave you with St. Francis and with a prayer attributed to him? It was quoted at the end of an announcement sent by a father and a mother who had just heard that one of their sons had been killed and the other was dangerously wounded. You can imagine what a grim day it must have been for them; but they, like so many countless others through ages found peace and comfort in the words of Francis, the Mirror of Christ, the little poor man who was surpassing rich, for here is the prayer:

Lord make me an instrument of Thy peace,
Where there is hate, may I bring love,
Where there is malice, may I bring pardon,
Where there is discord, may I bring harmony,
Where there is error, may I bring truth,
Where there is despair, may I bring hope,
Where there is darkness, may I bring light,
Where there is sadness, may I bring joy.
O Master, may I seek not so much to be comforted as to comfort,
To be understood as to understand, to be loved as to love;
For it is only in giving that we receive, in forgetting ourselves
    that we find,
In pardoning that we are pardoned in dying that we rise to
    eternal life.

Fourteen

Epilogue

If some of you feel that the story 'couldn't have happened', don't get too worried about that; for that was how everyone felt about it at the time.

But when they knew that it really HAD happened—well, you know what the result was: ordinary men changed into extraordinary men, timid men afraid when challenged to own that they knew Him, now willing, gladly, to die for Him. Only because they knew the story was true were they martyred and crucified and 'butchered to make a Roman holiday'. Men who a week before had sat behind locked doors, dazed and afraid and disillusioned, a week later had thrown their doors open to the world, faced crowds and kings, set out on dangerous journeys unafraid—filled now with a strange new confidence, speaking now with words that rang like steel.

They bore not the news of the world, but the news for the world; without fear and supremely happy they planned the conquest of the world—and all because of that first Easter day. 'But it doesn't make sense, man!' It's all right —that's what St. Thomas said too. But later he himself was martyred near Madras, near a place still called 'The Little Mound of St. Thomas', because he too saw that it made the only sense of an otherwise bewildering world.

Yes, it makes the only real sense. Had there been no first Easter Day, then the outlook would indeed have been grim. Because of Easter we know that right must triumph in the end; because of Easter we know that death itself is but another entrance into LIFE—a bend on the journey's road; because of Easter we know that the Lord of All Good Life is alive for evermore; and, as we sang—some of us—that Easter on an Italian battlefield in the sun, that great hymn 'O Valiant Hearts' to the fine tune by Harris:

> *Victor He rose; victorious, too, shall rise*
> *Those who have drunk his cup of sacrifice,*

each of us knew in our hearts that we meant it: for the good God has put into each one of us—yes, even into you and me—something of the risen glory and splendour of His Son.